MW00452613

# Morning Moments

## A Year of Cross Pointe

Sue Boldt

Unless otherwise noted, all scripture references are taken from the New King James Version®. Copyright © 1982 by Thomas Nelson. Used by permission. All rights reserved.

Scripture taken from the Amplified Bible (AMP), Copyright © 1954, 1958, 1962, 1964, 1965, 1987 by The Lockman Foundation. Used by permission.

Scripture quotations marked (NIV) are taken from the Holy Bible, New International Version®, NIV®. Copyright © 1973, 1978, 1984, 2011 by Biblica, Inc.™ Used by permission of Zondervan. All rights reserved worldwide. www.zondervan.com The "NIV" and "New International Version" are trademarks registered in the United States Patent and Trademark Office by Biblica, Inc.™

Any references to notes found in my personal Bible are from: *New Spirit Filled Life Bible*, Jack W. Hayford, Sr. Editor, (Nashville TN: Thomas Nelson, Inc., 2002)

Cover Design: *Alicen Curtis, i design*
Cover Photograph: *Sue Boldt, Old Oak Ranch, Sonora, CA*

Copyright © 2016 Sue Boldt
All rights reserved.
ISBN: 1540495485
ISBN-13: 9781540495488

# Dedication

This daily devotional is dedicated to
**Crossroads Church, Fairfield, CA**.
(now Home Church)
I love each one of you to pieces,
to the moon and beyond,
and with my whole heart.

All glory to the One who loves us beyond reason.

# Introduction...

I love the Lord Jesus.

Nope, I haven't always loved Him as completely or consistently, nor as ardently and lavishly as I should, that is for certain.

Yet, Jesus reached down into the messiness of my life and began a marvelous and miraculous work in me from the inside-out. His love has a way of doing that, you know. And once any of us get a taste of His Living Water – the limitless well of the Holy Spirit – we are pretty much wrecked for ordinary living. The extraordinary becomes the norm even in the most mundane of life's tasks. His presence makes our every step become holy ground.

Writing about Jesus is like candy for my soul. A treat, a joy, an overflow from the effervescent spring from within. For me, it is just dang fun! I think the All Creative God, loves it when we create. And we, who are birthed in His image, bring Him pleasure with any of our creative efforts no matter how lacking, childlike, or seemingly insignificant they are. This daily devotional is my attempt to share how God's Word is transforming my life, one day at a time, with the hope that your heart might come along for the ride.

You will notice that each day's short vignette provides an area for you to record your response to what the Lord is speaking into your life. However, these short writings are never meant to replace the power of knowing the Bible for yourself to bring the freedom, healing, guidance, and deliverance that only God can give *Psalm 107:20*. My prayer is for us both to *dig deeper into the* greater context of the verse given each day and discover the inexhaustible treasures of the Book of Books. And as we *read* His word, let's encounter the Living Word, King Jesus *John 1:14.*

# January 3

Many years ago, I sensed the Lord calling me to a deeper place in Him.

*O Lord, we have waited for You;*
*The desire of our soul is for Your name,*
*And for the remembrance of You.*
*With my soul I have desired You in the night,*
*Yes, by my spirit within me*
*I will seek You early.*
Isaiah 26:8b-9a

I responded about thirty years later. That was okay. Jesus was willing to wait for me. No, He wasn't waiting for me to get my act together; He was waiting for *me* to realize that *I* couldn't get my act together – without Him.

As you go through your day today, remember God is with you in your every step. He is right by you, indeed, *in* you. Look for His gifts in unexpected places. Be careful to respond to the prayer battles He calls you to in His name on behalf of others. Then, when you go night-night tonight, He will watch over you and give you a good morning kiss when you awake tomorrow.

What could be more amazing?

What Jesus is whispering to my heart today:

_____

_____

_____

_____

_____

# January 4

In the midst of this week and this New Year…

Should you have a sense of where God is taking you, yet you don't necessarily have all the *pieces of the picture* of *how* it will come about: keep your knees *planted* before His throne daily, look *up* and seek His face, and look *in* His word for daily direction. Your life's puzzle pieces will land exactly where the Lord Jesus wants them to in the order He has designed.
*Matthew 6:33*

Should Jesus be calling you to greater freedom from behaviors and lies you have believed about yourself (and Him), but you are frightened you will fail Him or that He might fail you, well, we are talking about the God of the Universe here! When you let Him, the Holy Spirit will take your hand and lead you out of the muck and mire of your mind, heart, and circumstances one step at a time.
*Psalm 40:2*

This is a week of new beginnings, hopes to be realized, and miracles to watch for. Keep your eyes open, your heart tender, and your mind from distraction. This week will be awesome in Jesus because He Who is in you is greater than anything!
*1 John 4:4*

What Jesus is whispering to my heart today:

_____

_____

_____

_____

_____

# January 9

For much of my life, I lived in the nagging insecurity of feeling *unseen*...

*Then she called the name of the LORD who spoke to her, You-Are-the-God-Who-Sees...*
Genesis 16:13

The enemy of my soul told me otherwise from this verse. He spoke subtle lies to me, and I gave him a toehold; I gave him the time of day, and he made it a stronghold. It is unfortunately so much easier to believe what the devil says, what the world says, and what my insecurities say instead of ruthlessly trusting Jesus' Words. For you too?

My desperate decision to live in the Lord's presence on a minute-by-minute basis broke up those lies. I began to recognize that the One and Only sees me, and He is the one who truly matters. Instead of the adversary's torment, Jesus' truth set me free. I discovered that the God of the Universe loves me, and He is absolutely crazy about me. And this gives me a reason to wake up in joy every single morning.

Now, your turn...

What Jesus is whispering to my heart today:

_____

_____

_____

_____

_____

# January 10

If you are still contemplating New Year's resolutions, here is a good one...

*He restores my soul;*
*He leads me in the paths of righteousness*
*For His name's sake.*
Psalm 23:3

The resolution? To keep surrendering full access to the Holy Spirit to restore our souls. In other words, asking Him to go deep in our hearts and minds to bring healing to our past, breaking lies we believe about ourselves and God, and delivering us from the grip of our enemy, the devil.

Take it from one who was once so tormented in her soul that she almost lost her family: an amazing husband and three beautiful children. In those dark days, I knew the heartache of brokenness, and now I know the pure bliss of freedom. Jesus is the real deal, and He can do it. He will be restoring us until our final breath, but we must start somewhere.

My *new* New Year's resolution? *Have at me, Lord.*

What Jesus is whispering to my heart today:

_____

_____

_____

_____

_____

# January 15

What a wonderfully well-worn and beloved Bible passage…

*Your word is a lamp to my feet,*
*And a light to my path.*
Psalm 119:105

Here we find His promise to give all the guidance we need, one footfall at a time. And, the great treasure is knowing each footstep we purpose in Him is one in front of the other for the long-range path of our lives.

Jesus' light is right here, right now, for what we face at this moment. Still, He gives glimpses of our destiny in Him. The trouble is, we want to jump from point A to point Q, missing out on all of the light-guided steps in between! We may try to hurry the path, jump over the track, or even skip the trail, but to what avail? We will miss the glory and power of the Holy Spirit and hearing His voice *every single* day of our lives.

So, it may be time to turn on the light. Let's spend some time basking in Jesus' presence today and drinking up His living, written Word.

And His gracious gift to us? The mundane will become extraordinary, the routine will become wonder-filled, and His light will dazzle our eyes *and* illuminate our steps.

What Jesus is whispering to my heart today:

_____

_____

_____

_____

_____

# January 16

The Book of Job hasn't always been a favorite of mine...

*I have heard of You by the hearing of the ear,*
*But now my eye sees You.*
Job 42:5

*The Book of Job for Dummies* is this: Satan accuses the Lord of protecting Job and gains the Lord's permission to *test* this man. Job loses children, possessions, and the respect of his wife and friends. Finally, he has catastrophic health issues. Think worst-case scenario on steroids.

There are literally *thirty-seven* chapters of anger, arguing, accusing, defending, whining, denial, and self-righteousness.

Then God shows up.

That's it. God, Himself, shows up. He asks a few questions, and Job comes to the one, and the only conclusion a person can come to - *God is the only thing that matters*. He is the bottom line to *everything*.

We desperately need to *see* God too. I don't know what you are facing, but *He* is the answer. No, not so much what He can *do* for you or me; rather, that HE *alone* is all we need. Enough said.

What Jesus is whispering to my heart today:

_____

_____

_____

_____

_____

# January 21

In my mid-thirties I suffered from moderate depression...

*...to give unto them beauty for ashes, the oil of joy for mourning, the garment of praise for the spirit of heaviness...*
Isaiah 61:3

The *spirit of heaviness* perfectly describes the dark and debilitating cloud over my life at that time. Yet, Jesus came to my rescue.

One Saturday morning while alone, the Holy Spirit spoke. I *saw* that I had allowed a demonic spirit of pride to take up residence in my heart and mind. I had thought my issues were rooted in worthlessness, not pride! Didn't I despise myself? Didn't I suffer from low self-esteem?

I now realize pride and shame usually walk hand-in-hand. Shame is at the core of most of our lives, yet to compensate for it, we try to *prove we are better than who we really think we are*. In this combustible combination, pride happens. That morning, the Holy Spirit dove deep into my soul, unlocking the pride and shame at the root of my obsession with appearance, insignificance, and dissatisfaction.

I confessed and renounced my sin of pride. Something left me, and the floodgates of heaven opened. I even experienced physical healing! He has a story for you too. Don't ever give up on Him.

What Jesus is whispering to my heart today:

_____

_____

_____

_____

# January 22

I have been making necklaces again. Mind you, I have no clue what I am doing. However, has that ever stopped me?

*For we are His workmanship,*
*created in Christ Jesus for good works,*
*which God prepared beforehand that we should walk in them.*
Ephesians 2:10

The Lord Almighty, the One and Only Creator placed within us is joy and desire *to be creative.* There is something so fulfilling when we get an idea – anything really – then make it happen. Honestly, He made in His image.

My friend, Cory Curry, relates that it took God only six days to speak into existence everything in this constantly enlarging and changing universe. However, it took Him *nine months* to carefully knit *you* together. No matter how you feel about yourself, to Him, you are a masterpiece, His most exceptional workmanship, His *poem* – the original Bible wording here.

If you are a little blue today, remember what you experience when you create something. Remember how much pleasure it brings your heart. And then recall t*his* is what God feels about *you* this very minute.

What Jesus is whispering to my heart today:

_____
_____
_____
_____
_____

# January 27

Jesus wants to bestow *double-back* what has been taken from you by your adversary...

*Instead of shame and dishonor, you will enjoy a double share of honor. You will possess a double portion of prosperity in your land, and everlasting joy will be yours.*
Isaiah 61:7

I encourage you to remember all the times when you have witnessed this happening. Think of those individuals who were once held captive to fear. Nevertheless, when the enemy's lies were exposed to King Jesus, how often the Lord now turns this person into a mighty and courageous warrior.

What about those persons who lived under a cloak of great shame, even from the womb? Have you noticed that when Jesus was invited to break these lies of worthlessness, He then transformed them into someone who knows their standing in heavenly places?

On and on this goes. So, what might be troubling you? Let Him have it. Give up control. Don't be afraid to be healed and delivered. Jesus will be gentle with you, but ruthless to Satan. You will be in good hands, and He will not fail you.

What Jesus is whispering to my heart today:

_____

_____

_____

_____

_____

# January 28

Living in this day and age is not for the faint of heart...

*There is no fear in love; but perfect love casts out fear, because fear involves torment. But he who fears has not been made perfect in love.*
1 John 4:18

Nevertheless, the Bible tells us there really isn't anything new taking place: war, famine, hatred, violence, and destruction. Simply read the Old and New Testament and compare their accounts of distress with any news story of today. So...

Our only hope is in the Lord Jesus Christ. He is truly everything. Eternity is real, and it is just a breath away. Comprehending this truth is either exhilarating news or the most frightening; it all depends on where your heart and mind are abiding, living, and dwelling.

Right this moment, I choose Jesus. I prefer to trust Him. The Bible tells me that His perfect love casts out all fear *1 John 4:18*. And, the minute fear is gone, heaven breaks through to reveal even more of God. More of His peace, His power, His incredible joy, and His intentional, intimate love for each one of us.

I choose Jesus. He alone has my mind and heart. I actively choose to trust Him. Will you join me?

What Jesus is whispering to my heart today:

_____

_____

_____

_____

_____

# February 2

You are the apple of His eye...

*Keep me as the apple of Your eye;*
*Hide me under the shadow of Your wings.*
*Psalm 17:8*

Did you know, did you realize that God Almighty only ever thinks
about *YOU*? His Word tells us He only thinks loving, kind, respectful,
cherishing, exquisitely lovely, good, purposeful thoughts about you
always. His thoughts of you in any given moment outnumber the grains
of sand on the seashore.

You are the *apple* of His eye. Quite literally, you are the *pupil* of His eye.
You know, the black dot in the middle? In other words, He only
sees *you* as a lover only sees the object of His affection.

If you have cause to doubt this ageless truth at this moment, well, it is
time to get back to His Word. His unfailing, Truth-filled Word. It is time
to carve a niche of your life to be alone with King Jesus the *Living Word*.
He wants to remind you that you are everything to Him.

Because you, dear one, are all He sees.

What Jesus is whispering to my heart today:

_____

_____

_____

_____

_____

# February 3

Have you ever felt held captive to your life's situation?

There have been times when I have absolutely felt captive to my surroundings, my position in life, or vocation. Honestly, I have believed I was needed more elsewhere. Or rather, I wanted to be somewhere else...

*And seek the peace of the city where I have caused you to be carried away captive, and pray to the LORD for it; for in its peace you will have peace.*
Jeremiah 29:7

Nevertheless, God nailed me with these verses initially given to the Hebrews in captivity, and I took them to heart. I started praying for my current situation – my workplace. Now, almost daily, I get the opportunity to minister to five to ten people about Jesus. It is crazy what the Holy Spirit is doing in this place of my *captivity*.

So, start praying for those in the area where you may sometimes feel held captive. And receive the promise found just a few verses later...

*For I know the thoughts that I think toward you, says the LORD, thoughts of peace and not of evil, to give you a future and a hope.*
Jeremiah 29:11

What Jesus is whispering to my heart today:

_____

_____

_____

_____

_____

# February 8

In the midst of this week...

Should you feel confused, distraught, or caught in a quandary, look to Him, who is the Alpha and Omega. He is the only one who knows the beginning, middle, and best outcome. Let *Him* direct your steps and lean wholly into His arms.
*Revelation 1:8*

Should you be exhausted, weary, and just plain pooped out, come sit beside the still waters. That means stopping busyness as soon as possible and heading to a quiet place – like the bathroom if you have small children – and let His Word refresh you. Turn to some of your favorite passages and allow the Holy Spirit who wrote them to breathe His reviving wind into your heart and mind.
*Psalm 23:2*

This is a week of new beginnings, hopes to be realized, and miracles to watch for. Keep your eyes open, your heart tender, and your mind from distraction. This week will be awesome in Jesus because He Who is in you is greater than anything!
*1 John 4:4*

What Jesus is whispering to my heart today:

_____

_____

_____

_____

_____

# February 9

Ouch!

*No discipline is enjoyable while it is happening--it's painful! But afterward there will be a peaceful harvest of right living for those who are trained in this way.*
Hebrews 12:11

Yes, He is saying some difficult things to me in his gentle, but firm voice. He is speaking these words because He loves me. If you read further, the writer of the Book of Hebrews explains this further.

Still, it is hard to hear these words from His lips, yet my joy in Jesus is returning. You know, the kind of happiness not based on sweet circumstances, but the celebration of freedom from some junk that was starting to overtake my life. I had wondered where my joy in the river of the Holy Spirit had gone. So…

Don't be afraid to hear and face some stuff in your soul. He is at work, releasing you from selfishness, self-centeredness, self-will, self-righteousness – all the *self* stuff. I am right there with you in this. And the best part of all? He promises to replace these broken, rebellious areas in us with the best *self* of all – *Himself.*

What Jesus is whispering to my heart today:

_____

_____

_____

_____

_____

# February 14

I am so moved by these words that celebrate love...

*I will betroth you to Me forever; Yes, I will betroth you to Me in
righteousness and justice, In lovingkindness and mercy; I will betroth
you to Me in faithfulness, And you shall know the LORD.*
Hosea 2:19-20

Jesus is forever and foremost after my heart and affections. He is not so
much interested in what I *do* for Him or how *much* I accomplish for His
Kingdom. Those things are of much lesser value and will naturally fall
into place when I am walking with Him in *first love*. He is after
my *complete affection*.

What matters most to Him is a heart like King David. *"I will seek your
beauty..."* And like Mary, of Mary and Martha fame, *"She has desired
the one thing..."* as she merely sat at His feet to hear His voice.

Let's give Him our hearts today, holding nothing back. Let's love Him
with all that is within us and make Him alone the object of all of our
affection and delight. Then, our hearts will always be safely hidden in the
wonder of His infinite, incomparable, beyond-comprehension love.

What Jesus is whispering to my heart today:

_____

_____

_____

_____

_____

# February 15

In the midst of this week…

Should you suffer a sudden loss in a relationship, a job, finances, security, or a loved one, look up! Your redemption is near! Don't let the enemy scatter and distract you in your thoughts. You need more than ever to trust the One Who loves you beyond reason. He *is* greater than your loss, and He *is* the only one who can help you through this. Dive deep into His Word and into His presence.
*Psalm 34:17-18*

Should you have a disappointment – something or someone didn't come through for you as you had hoped – maybe, just maybe, the Lord is using this to get your attention that He alone needs to be your expectation. He knows what He is doing, even when others don't seem to!
*Luke 12:32*

This is a week of new beginnings, hopes to be realized, and miracles to watch for. Keep your eyes open, your heart tender, and your mind from distraction. This week will be awesome in Jesus because He Who is in you is greater than anything!
*1 John 4:4*

What Jesus is whispering to my heart today:

_____

_____

_____

_____

_____

# February 16

One of our daughters called today with excitement ringing in her voice.

*Therefore do not be like them. For your Father knows the things you have need of before you ask Him.*
Matthew 6:8

Today, for Shiloh and her a family of five, the Lord had come through as He always does.

The answer had come after months of prayer, literally up to the deadline of their great need to find a new residence. Yes, we knew the Lord would be faithful to them – my husband and I have a ton of Jesus/house stories. Nevertheless, a lot of nice homes, even seemingly perfect homes for them, had come and gone to others.

I started with great faith concerning our kids' dilemma, however, as time progressed and days became numbered, panic-praying took over. Do you know what I mean? Yet, when has God ever failed to provide for us? I remember the passage above. Enough said. God's peace began ruling instead.

Whatever you are facing, He already knows about it. Take a look at the verses surrounding *Matthew 6:8* and place your concerns confidently in His hands and *trust*.

What Jesus is whispering to my heart today:

_____

_____

_____

_____

_____

# February 17

The opening question is asked...

*Who has measured the waters in the hollow of His hand, or with the breadth of His hand marked off the heavens?*
Isaiah 40:12a

When we consider who the Lord is and that He uses the span of His mighty fingers to measure the untold galaxies, immeasurable light-years away in the distance? And yet, I am reminded of the prophet's words a few chapters later...

*...In the shadow of His hand He has hidden Me.*
Isaiah 49:2a

Our amazing, unfathomable God not only holds all of the oceans and stars in the single palm of His mighty hand, He holds *me* there too. And, our God holds *you* there as well – tenderly, carefully, purposefully, and powerfully – in the cup of His eternal hand.

Rest in this knowledge. Rest in His care. Rest in the safety and strength of this truth.

What Jesus is whispering to my heart today:

_____

_____

_____

_____

_____

# February 18

If the Christian's strength is the joy of the Lord, it is not rocket science to realize our adversary will go after this source of our might in Christ.

*You will show me the path of life;*
*In Your presence is fullness of joy;*
*At Your right hand are pleasures forevermore.*
Psalm 16:11

I have been a Christian for a long time. I don't know it all or have it all together. However, I have experienced the Holy Spirit, overflowing with buckets-full and drenching to-and-through the skin with *joy,* when I make room for time in God's presence. Often.

So, any time, any amount of time – whether short or lengthy – set aside time to bask in the Lord's presence. Feasting upon His Word will always be opposed by the devil. If your soul's enemy can separate you from time spent with the Almighty, the battle for other areas of your life will almost surely fall his way.

No, this isn't a time for a guilt-trip. It is a call to keep your joy in Jesus full to the brim by cultivating and nurturing your strength *in Him* because the joy you will experience in His presence alone can never be lost, no matter what happens in your life.

What Jesus is whispering to my heart today:

_____

_____

_____

_____

_____

# February 19

Have we been *giving place* to anything lately?

*...nor give place to the devil.*
Ephesians 4:27

The original Greek word used for '*place*' here is **topos**. It is the root word defining *topography*, *geography*, or *location* in our English language. Paul is advising us not to give *ground* to our adversary. He is telling us not to give the enemy an inch; because he will take a mile.

Where is this *place*? It is the realm of our soul: our hearts and minds. When we allow the enemy entry to our thoughts and emotions, he loves to take ground and set up a stronghold – an unshakeable grip – on our thoughts, our actions, and our responses, causing addictions and bondage. We become powerless to break his *strong hold* in us no matter how hard we try. But, enough talk about the evil one.

Let's talk about the overwhelming love and power of the One and Only Who came to destroy every work of the devil. *1 John 3:8*

So, don't give up. Pursue the Lord. Seek Spirit-filled help and let His Word bring healing. Freedom may come in an instant, or you may gain back ground one inch at a time. Nevertheless, your release will happen. Deliverance is yours in Jesus' name.

What Jesus is whispering to my heart today:

_____

_____

_____

_____

_____

# February 20

Leaving eternal footprints…

*How beautiful upon the mountains*
*Are the feet of him who brings good news,*
*Who proclaims peace,*
*Who brings glad tidings of good things,*
*Who proclaims salvation,*
*Who says to Zion, "Your God reigns!"*
Isaiah 52:7

Every day it seems I take a lot of steps: steps around the busy medical clinic I work at, steps through my favorite market, and steps along my neighborhood as I attempt to jog. Steps, yes, steps. Lots of them.

God's Word tells me that I have the potential to leave eternal footsteps, and this speaks to my heart. I want every step I take to count. I want to walk where He is leading me to walk and seize the everlasting opportunities the Holy Spirit places all around me.

Yes. Everywhere I go, may my steps, actions, prayers, thoughts, and words proclaim: my God reigns!

Want to join me?

What Jesus is whispering to my heart today:

_____

_____

_____

_____

_____

# February 21

For you were once...

*For you were once darkness, but now you are light in the Lord. Walk as children of light.*
Ephesians 5:8

Paul writes in the past tense, *you were once* darkness, but you aren't aligned with the dark's depravity anymore. You are now walking in God's light; this is already accomplished and already done. There are countless past tense verses like this in God's Word.

You know, all of the world's religions or attempts to reach God are based upon *effort*. I get this. For years as a Christian, I kept *doing* and almost always failing. You too? However, the crazy thing is, the very moment we received Christ by faith *John 1:12,* the cross and resurrection did away with our need to perform. When we gave our lives to Him, God placed and positioned us in the Kingdom of the Son of His love.

Our new home is in Christ. We no longer need to try and to grasp for something that is already ours. If you are struggling in any area of your life, remember that you are *already* light in the Lord. Even if the world, the devil, and your mind are telling you otherwise. Your position in Him is your starting point and the source of your victory. Come and stand on this *launching pad.*

What Jesus is whispering to my heart today:

_____

_____

_____

_____

_____

# February 26

You know, salvation really *is* powerful.

*And Jesus said to him, "Today salvation has come to this house, because he also is a son of Abraham;"*
Luke 19:9

Zacchaeus turned from a lifetime of fraudulence to follow Jesus at great personal cost and comfort. He held nothing back – making a radical decision to let God's Spirit do a grand, far-reaching overhaul of his life *and* his home.

Salvation (Greek – **Soteria**) Meaning: *Deliverance, preservation, soundness, prosperity, happiness, rescue, general well-being. The word is used in a material/temporal sense; and a spiritual/eternal purpose.*

I have a friend who is taking a stand for the Lord's salvation in her home: her children, her marriage, herself. It has been thrilling and challenging all at the same time. It has been liberating and sometimes so greatly opposed by the flesh and the devil, she has often despaired. Yet, this once broken, unhealthy, and oppressed family is being *saved*.

My point is: Let's all stand for salvation and health in our *homes*. We *will* be opposed, and it *will be uncomfortable*. However, Jesus' salvation for our families is worth it, oh so worth it. And, it must start with *us*.

What Jesus is whispering to my heart today:

_____

_____

_____

_____

_____

# February 27

I just received news that a long-time friend of ours has suffered a significant heart attack. I am prompted to pray God's Word boldly...

*He sent His word and healed them,*
*And delivered them from their destructions.*
Psalms 107:20

I know this may sound like just mere hocus-pocus, but it isn't. I am living proof. Not only that I am still alive today from being diagnosed with Stage 4 incurable cancer, but even more, I *know* it was the power of God's Word that brought complete freedom from the bondages and addictions of my life.

The Bible is powerful and alive *Hebrews 4:12-13*. This written Word reveals the Living Word, the Lord Jesus Christ *John 1:14*. Our mustard seed faith mingled with the power of His Word topples the enemy's strongholds, crushes hell's advancement, and speaks healing to every area of our lives.

Pray for a greater hunger to know God's Word for yourself. I am praying for this, too. There is a broken and dying world out there longing to see men and women who are passionate about a living God, speaking a living Word, and living extraordinary lives for His glory.

What Jesus is whispering to my heart today:

_____

_____

_____

_____

_____

# March 3

A little word association here. The word is *journaling...*

*Thus speaks the LORD God of Israel, saying: "Write in a book for yourself all the words that I have spoken to you."*
Jeremiah 30:2

*Argghhhhh* we may think. It takes time. Why bother? Who cares?

*Guilt.* I always give up after I miss a few days. I have ten million journals around the house that I have started. I can't find a user-friendly app.

*Bliss.* Yes, it is messy. It takes time, but it keeps me accountable. Journaling helps me remember what God has spoken to me, done for me, and what He has promised me.

I'm praying this will give you a gentle, but firm kick in the rear to record His thoughts to you by whatever means you choose—handwritten, word-processed, graffiti, sidewalk chalk. Okay, maybe not graffiti.

The point is to remember by processing your thoughts with His. Keeping a journal will keep you focused, helping you to look back, and looking forward. Consider keeping a written record. You will get the hang of it, and you will be blessed.

What Jesus is whispering to my heart today:

_____

_____

_____

_____

_____

# March 4

I want to stay desperate for God.

*Then those who went before warned him that he should be quiet; but he cried out all the more, "Son of David, have mercy on me!"*
Luke 18:39

Right now, life is good. Our bills are paid, and the kids are behaving themselves. Our church is growing a bit, I have a steady job, and my CT scans are still clear. Food is on the table, and I get to live indoors. It would be so easy to *coast*.

But no. I don't want to. I am happiest and most fulfilled when I live life on the edge of my seat, desperate for Jesus.

I don't want to be quiet. I don't want to follow or listen to the crowd. I want to be like the man in this passage. I want to cry out to my Savior all the more, because…

Even though I am doing very well, others aren't. They don't need me; they need Jesus *in* me. And so, I want to stay desperate for God because quite honestly, there is no high like the Most High, and no Savior like the One and Only. Yes, I want to stay desperate for Him.

What Jesus is whispering to my heart today:

_____

_____

_____

_____

_____

# March 9

Been there. Done that...

*For this is the love of God, that we keep His commandments.*
*And His commandments are not burdensome.*
1 John 5:3

When our lives feel heavy, our prayers powerless, our time in the Word lackluster, or the sense of His presence only a memory, we have taken a detour somewhere. Usually, a detour from His *grace*. And His *love*.

It's hard to imagine the words *grace* and *commandment*s in the same sentence. Nevertheless, they belong together. What are Jesus' commandments? He tells us to love Him first and everybody else the way we want to be loved. When this is difficult or a burden, we are trying to live in and for Him by our own strength. Pure and simple.

So. If you are reading this and you are feeling guilt, heaviness, shame, discouragement, or less-than; well, just knock it off! Really. Don't receive these lies from the pit. Because...

*For if our heart condemns us, God is greater than our heart, and knows all things.* 1 John 3:20

It is time to take a load off at the feet of King Jesus.

What Jesus is whispering to my heart today:

_____

_____

_____

_____

# March 10

Nobody can do it for us – must carry our own shield...

*...above all, taking the shield of faith with which you will be able to quench all the fiery darts of the wicked one.*
Ephesians 6:16

Faith is a growing process for sure, but the Scriptures speak toward two paths to greater belief...

One: Know His Word inside-out-and-backward. His Holy Spirit breathed Word ignites the flame of faith in our soul and spirit like nothing else can. We need to endeavor to be soaked, drenched, and saturated in the Word for *ourselves*; without guilt and with a new translation!

Two: Know the Author of the Bible inside-out-and-backward. It is hard to trust someone you don't know personally. Find yourself in His presence alone, under the shadow of His wings, as often as possible.

At the end of the day, let this piece of our armor – the shield of faith in Him – be the one we lift high and effortlessly.

The devil's darts will drop to the ground.

What Jesus is whispering to my heart today:

_____

_____

_____

_____

_____

# March 15

Plain and simple, this is a cry from the depths of a hungry heart...

*Whom have I in heaven but You?*
*And there is none upon earth that I desire besides You.*
Psalm 73:25

This psalmist has tasted all that life on this planet has to offer, but he knows – I mean really knows – there is only One worth pursuing. Oh yes. I can agree with these words.

However, God would say to us...

*"Whom have I in heaven but you, dear child?*
*And there is none upon earth that I desire more than you."*

No matter what we have done.
No matter what we haven't done.
No matter how we have lived or allowed death into our lives.
No matter our mistakes and stumbles or our flaws and failures.

He desires us. He holds nothing back to bring us to Himself. Let's stop the struggle to do life in our own strength and run into His embrace. Now.

What Jesus is whispering to my heart today:

_____

_____

_____

_____

_____

# March 16

I think King Jesus might be a foodie...

I mean, really. We find Him in the scriptures always eating with someone. In all four Gospels, we find Him feeding thousands. We see Him break bread with a tax collector. He takes great care preparing for His final meal before the cross and after rising from the dead. He even cooks up breakfast for the guys!

I just looked up the definition of *foodie*. Webster's states that it is someone who enjoys and cares about food very much. Hmmmm. Well, on second thought. Maybe it is not so much the meal where Lord Jesus finds enjoyment and care; it is the company He invites.

*Behold, I stand at the door and knock. If anyone hears My voice and opens the door, I will come in to him and dine with him, and he with Me.*
Revelation 3:20

This verse wrecks me every time.

Jesus is after me. And you. It is the pleasure of our company He is after. It is our care He comes to provide. He is knocking on our hearts to dine with us. I think it is time to open the door.

What Jesus is whispering to my heart today:

_____

_____

_____

_____

_____

# March 21

In the midst of this week...

Should you find yourself in circumstances that seem overwhelming and entirely out of your control, the Lord wants you to really know and experience His work on your behalf in amazing ways. You will know Him as *El Shaddai* – Almighty God.
*Genesis 17:1*

Should you find yourself having physical difficulties, either sickness or injury, Jesus wants you to really know and experience Him as *Jehovah Rapha* – the God Who Heals.
*Exodus 15:26*

Should you find yourself perplexed, confused, or discouraged, the Lord wants you to really know and experience Him as the Peace that passes all understanding – *Jehovah Shalom*.
*Isaiah 9:6*

This is a week of new beginnings, hopes to be realized, and miracles to watch for. Keep your eyes open, your heart tender, and your mind from distraction. This week will be awesome in Jesus because He Who is in you is greater than anything!
*1 John 4:4*

What Jesus is whispering to my heart today:

_____

_____

_____

_____

_____

# March 22

We sometimes miss God's Promised Land in our lives when...

- we think we know better than Him and His Word
- we think He is holding out on us
- we think He is working too slowly
- we don't really trust His beyond-reason love for us
- we want to do, what we want to do

*...the children of Benjamin did not drive out the Jebusites who inhabited Jerusalem..."* Judges 1:21

What really struck my heart was the note in my study Bible:
*This provides an account of Israel's failure to complete the conquest of the Promised Land as the Lord commanded them.*

Is it challenging to possess our Promised Land? I don't believe it always must be. Think of walking with Jesus under an umbrella. You *gotta* hold tight to Him, or you will come out from under His covering. When He goes left, you go left. When He goes right, you go right. In every battle, and every situation.

Will the world and the enemy splash you at times? Yes. Though *close* to Him, He will cover you from, through, and in a downpour. He loves you. Knowing His Word will only strengthen your grip on His umbrella. It is time to come out of the rain and into His land of Promise.

What Jesus is whispering to my heart today:

_____

_____

_____

_____

# March 27

The Greatest Story Ever Told is truly the story of God's rescue mission.

*The thief does not come except to steal, and to kill, and to destroy.*
*I have come that they may have life,*
*and that they may have it more abundantly.*
John 10:10

When Jesus clothed Himself in human flesh, He was making an invasion behind enemy lines *1 John 5:19*, to rescue us. Yes, to rescue us from the domain of satan to whom the first couple handed over their God-given dominion of the earth when they were in the Garden.

Jesus also came to snatch us from the miry pits we often find ourselves in due to our own selfish and destructive choices. Adding to the fallout from our own paths of pain, are also the issues, hang-ups, and hurts that have come to us through the generations of our family, and the hard-knocks of our environment.

So, in what area of your life do you need Jesus' rescue? Ask yourself honestly. Then, ask Him honestly – to deliver you.

Yes, the Lord Jesus is enough. He is more than enough. His rescue is your destiny, and His abundance is your portion because of His glorious grace. He is waiting for you to reach out and take hold of His hand of freedom.

What Jesus is whispering to my heart today:

_____

_____

_____

_____

# March 28

In the midst of this week…

Should you receive some difficult news about a loved one
– like I just did a minute ago – stop and wait on the Lord. You are not
defenseless. You have the Holy Spirit living inside of you. It is time to
quiet your heart and mind and lean into the Commander of Heaven's
Hosts. Pray what you know. Pray what you sense He is telling you. Pray
in the Spirit. You have the resources of heaven working on your behalf.
Now stand and trust.
*Psalm 46:10*

Should you suddenly be confused about an area of your life, beat it back
to God's Word. Beat it back to the last thing the Lord spoke to your heart
about this situation. The enemy is probably trying to distract you.
Enough said.
*Psalm 119:105*

This is a week of new beginnings, hopes to be realized, and miracles to
watch for. Keep your eyes open, your heart tender, and your mind from
distraction. This week will be awesome in Jesus because He Who is in
you is greater than anything!
*1 John 4:4*

What Jesus is whispering to my heart today:

_____

_____

_____

_____

_____

# April 2

His finished work on the cross was *our* beginning...

*So when Jesus had received the sour wine, He said, "It is finished!" And bowing His head, He gave up His spirit.*
John 19:30

On the platform of this simple phrase – *It is finished!* – we stand in the power of God's Word that our sin is forgiven; our spiritual, emotional, and physical healing purchased; freedom is our portion; the enemy has been completely vanquished, and heaven has been secured for us.

I am ALL about feeling, sensing, and experiencing the presence and power of God in our lives. Nevertheless, there are times when we have to ruthlessly stand on the truth of God's Word, which proclaims that Jesus' death and resurrection finished all the *unfinished* business in our lives. No matter what we are feeling.

Whatever is causing you anguish, anxiety, fear, or possibly guilt, Jesus has already *finished it*–whatever *it* is you need. Stand on this truth, not your feelings. Take your hands completely off the predicament you currently face and give it to the One and Only who purchased your full redemption and healing. Wait to see what He does. Because, *it is finished!*

What Jesus is whispering to my heart today:

_____

_____

_____

_____

_____

# April 3

The weight of the cross hit me today while serving on jury duty...

*But this Man, after He had offered one sacrifice for sins forever,*
*sat down at the right hand of God,*
 Hebrews 10:12

Being in this situation, at a courthouse and soon to be sitting in sight of
the judge's desk, brings home the reality of Jesus' horrific and
unimaginable sacrifice for me. I was found guilty. I stood before the
righteous Judge of the Universe, and I was found wanting. Treason
against the Holy One. My crime? Rebellion. The sentence pronounced
was death.

Yet, on Good Friday so long ago, the Judge Who had every right to pass
sentence on me, took off His robes, stepped down from His elevated,
most high and holy platform and stood in front of me. Then He took the
death penalty. For me.

So, I could go free. Pardoned completely. Forgiven absolutely.

Oh, the story of the cross. I will never earn this freedom and pardon; nor
is there anything in me which could have brought it about. It was and is
God's love alone. I never want to forget this.

What Jesus is whispering to my heart today:

_____
_____
_____
_____
_____

# April 8

I love our adorable grandchildren, however...

*For everyone who partakes only of milk is unskilled in the word of*
*righteousness, for he is a babe.*
Hebrews 5:13

Oh! To keep them in their sweet innocent ages forever where everything
is a wonder and each day is a new adventure to discover! However, if
they stayed at their ages for years on end, something would be dreadfully
wrong. As much as we want them to stay little, we would never wish for
their growth to be stunted or stalled. What a tragedy that would be.

How many of us are still in the baby stage of our walk with the Lord?
Fears still taunt us, peace eludes us, and our love for others is careful and
unsure. We find strongholds have only become stronger, faith is still a
theory, and the power of the gospel is tepid at best. Our Bibles are dusty,
our knees aren't worn out, and our hands lay limp at our sides.

God calls us to be childlike, but not childish. I want to walk in wonder
and discovery every single day in the magnitude of Jesus' love.
Nevertheless, I want to be a continually maturing, Spirit-filled believer. I
choose to press forward for all that He has for me. Will you join me?


What Jesus is whispering to my heart today:

_____

_____

_____

_____

_____

# April 9

Years ago, a friend gave me five-dozen, long-stemmed roses...

There were so many of these blush-hued beauties, and I gave several away. However, there were still several of these breath-taking blooms left. I had no adequate vase to put them in, just a large mayonnaise jar.

*But we have this treasure in jars of clay to show that this all-surpassing power is from God and not from us.*
2 Corinthians 4:7

The roses were given to me just before the Holy Spirit orchestrated a tremendous breakthrough in my life. At the time, I was still struggling with some deeply embedded strongholds in my soul. Yet, one day the Lord spoke to me as I rounded the table displaying my gift of roses...

**Sweetheart, what do you see?**
  *Such beautiful, perfect roses. They are stunning, Lord.*
**You don't see the mayonnaise jar do you?**
  *No, no – I only see the splendor of such beauty.*
**It is the same for you when you fully surrender to Me. People will see My beauty overflowing your jar of clay. Are you ready?**

*Are you ready too?*

What Jesus is whispering to my heart today:

_____

_____

_____

_____

_____

# April 14

The whole of Hebrews 10 is one of the *classics*...

*Then I said, 'Behold, I have come -*
*In the volume of the book it is written of Me -*
*To do Your will, O God.'*
Hebrews 10:7

In this chapter, the writer settles forever the absolute, unfailing, and incomprehensible depth and power of Jesus' sacrifice to eradicate our sin and clothe us with His righteousness.

What speaks to me in this moment is knowing what Jesus' personal sacrifice was to leave heaven's incomparable splendor, become a mere man, and bear my sin. He endured the unimaginable agony of separation from the Father and the Holy Spirit as He took my iniquity upon Himself. He did this to save and redeem a worthless, unholy particle of dust – me.

Jesus, fully God, co-eternal, co-divine, co-existent, co-equal with the Father and Holy Spirit, well, chose to do the Father's will. Choosing to leave perfect harmony, love, union, and fellowship within the Godhead, He fulfilled the Father's request to bring us home so we might share in their love relationship John 15:9-17.

What an inestimable gift.

What Jesus is whispering to my heart today:

_____

_____

_____

_____

# April 15

For years – I mean years – I planted the world's way of thinking into my soul: my heart and my mind…

*I (The LORD) said, 'Plant the good seeds of righteousness, and you will harvest a crop of love. Plow up the hard ground of your hearts, for now is the time to seek the LORD, that he may come and shower righteousness upon you.*
Hosea 10:12 NLT (parentheses, mine)

Yes, most certainly, I loved the Lord Jesus. Nevertheless, the stuff of the world, you know, self-seeking, appearance, possessions, and the enemy's definition of success, captured me.

I allowed the lies of the world to rule me through media, my brokenness, even the church at times. These lies robbed me of the truth that Jesus is all I need or want, that His presence and His Word are the only fountains of life filled with significance and purpose.

Still, lies are so much easier to believe. Just read a few verses further in Hosea to see this. It takes faith to trust God fully. But oh, when we do, we harvest a crop of His lavish love that makes us whole.
Now is the time to seek the LORD. Let's open up and let Him pour in.

What Jesus is whispering to my heart today:

_____
_____
_____
_____
_____

# April 16

My husband has a favorite phrase: *I love to stop stuff!* In other words, know when it is time to end an endeavor. Solomon seems to agree...

*Don't wear yourself out trying to get rich.*
*Be wise enough to know when to quit.*
Proverbs 23:4 NLT

No, I am not giving you license to quit your marriage or give up on your family members! I am talking about whatever is running you ragged – those business, ministry, even a kitchen-remodel-type-endeavors – because *He is not in it.* It may be time to examine your heart, your motives, and the real reason you are wearing yourself out for something that feels dry as a bone.

Yes. So much of the Scripture tells us to persevere, endure, and be steadfast. Nevertheless, there are times when the Holy Spirit is just trying to get through to us that *enough is enough.*

So. If this is for you, go to prayer. Wait for Him. Hear Him. If this doesn't speak to you currently, I'll bet you know someone it does. Maybe it's time to have a loving heart-to-heart and go to Him in prayer together. Stopping something is never easy, but the new, open doors He brings are oh so delightful.

What Jesus is whispering to my heart today:

_____

_____

_____

_____

_____

# April 17

*Don't force it!* Growing up, my dad often spoke these words to me...

*...Let it be to me according to your word...*
Luke 1:38

Whenever I was trying to fix something, jiggle loose a piece of a broken
toy, or I simply was impatient, I remember hearing those words. I hear
the voice of my *Heavenly Father* speaking the same words to me from
the story of Jesus' birth as I consider how God arranged all the puzzle
pieces of this event without help from anyone. His perfect timing; the
miracles and impossibilities realized.

There are times when we need to wait for His timing. There are seasons
when we need to release how we think things in our lives should take
place in exchange for God's out-of-the-box thinking. Yes, we are often
called to press through to obtain what God has promised us and contend
for His will in the midst of adversity. Yet, *sometimes*, we may be told
*don't force it* and let Him have full reign.

If the Lord has spoken a specific word to you, it may be time to let it rest
in His hands. He will complete that which He has started. It's time to say,
*Let it be to me according to your word,* and see what He births in your
next adventure in Him. It will be amazing...

What Jesus is whispering to my heart today:

_____

_____

_____

_____

_____

# April 18

In the midst of this week…

Whatever you face this week – big or little, tiny or looming – the Lord of Heaven's Armies has your back! He surrounds you completely, so lean hard into Him. He is the best defensive line you could ever have!
*Isaiah 139:5-6*

If you have been hesitant to step out in a new direction in your life and you are uncertain as to what you should do, slowly start moving forward in what you think you are hearing the Lord say to you. It is much easier to guide something that is in motion than something at a dead stop. Don't let the enemy paralyze you, telling you that you will make a mistake. Carefully lay everything before the Lord, then start moving forward.
*Isaiah 43:18-19*

This is a week of new beginnings, hopes to be realized, and miracles to watch for. Keep your eyes open, your heart tender, and your mind from distraction. This week will be awesome in Jesus because He Who is in you is greater than anything!
*1 John 4:4*

What Jesus is whispering to my heart today:

_____

_____

_____

_____

# April 19

I just experienced something wonder-filled...

*For God so loved the world that He gave His only begotten Son, that whoever believes in Him should not perish but have everlasting life.* John 3:16

Just now, I came from a meeting with a brand-new believer in Jesus. We have been meeting in that great discipleship gathering place: MickyD's. This lovely forty-something woman just now read *John 3:16* for the very first time in her life.

This verse, containing the whole of the gospel, never loses its *punch*. It never loses its *tenderness*. The heart of God was poured out for His wayward children. For God so loved.

Two things: Who do you have in your life that needs someone to walk with them in their faith journey, either *to* Jesus or *in* Jesus?

And second, don't these precious and most powerful words from this verse say it all? He came for me. He came for you. That is all we need to know and always remember.

What Jesus is whispering to my heart today:

_____

_____

_____

_____

_____

# April 20

Yes, it is often the little things that trip us up...

*Catch us the foxes,*
*The little foxes that spoil the vines,*
*For our vines have tender grapes.*
Song of Songs 2:15

I'm pretty good at trusting God for the big things in life. Yet today, when a little distraction came up, I found my heart and mind frantically trying to – you know – help Him out. Ever done that? I wanted to help the Lord out because I could. I could manipulate things to my advantage, my desires, and my wants. Yet, do I really want that?

It was good, rich, right, and joyful to put this small matter back where it belonged – hidden in Him. What a relief! Because, honestly, the little things do matter. And, I, for one, don't want to live less-than because I think I know better. Do you have a little thing to hand over to the Master?

What Jesus is whispering to my heart today:

_____

_____

_____

_____

_____

# April 21

It is time to forgive. With those words, possibly some names are going through your mind and heart...

*And forgive us our debts,*
*As we forgive our debtors.*
Matthew 6:12

Some of these folks you are thinking of may have incurred horrendous hurt and harm to you, either mentally, emotionally, or physically. It seems impossible to forgive them. However, in the power of the Holy Spirit, the Lord will help you to release their *debt* to you. This may take place little-by-little. One peel-back of the onion-like shell of unforgiveness at a time. And yes, it may take time, but Jesus has all the time in the world. You have to start somewhere.

If you have been around Jesus for a while, you know forgiveness is the heart of the gospel. Forgiveness is His heart – *always*. So take some time now, not later. Begin by speaking their names in your thoughts before the Lord and asking for His help. He will not fail you. He will begin bringing release, healing, and redemption, but it starts with you saying a simple, *Yes, I am ready, Lord.*

What Jesus is whispering to my heart today:

_____

_____

_____

_____

_____

# April 26

To live purposefully...

*But Daniel purposed in his heart that he would not defile himself with the portion of the king's delicacies...*
Daniel 1:8

Several years ago, our adult son rejected Christ. He was on a quest for truth that involved separating from his beautiful wife. He was *sure* the *truth* was *not* Jesus. Hard stuff for his parents.

We went to battle for his soul. Using the authority given to us by King Jesus in *Luke 10:17-20*, our family went into battle prayer against the lying, deceiving spirits that were blinding our son's eyes. Isaiah 35 was our God-given battle plan in prayer.

I bring this up because at that time, I *purposed*, with my heart and mind, to not let *anything* distract me from the Lord. For me, that meant media distraction and wasting time with stuff that really *didn't matter*. I had a lot of that in my life. The adversary's defeat took place about three months later when Jeremy met Jesus. Our God is *so* good.

Is it time for you to be *purposeful* about something in your life? Do not neglect His voice because He has a miracle in store. And then, you will want to live this way forever.

What Jesus is whispering to my heart today:

_____

_____

_____

_____

_____

# April 27

I believe the Lord gave me a visual...

*I am the vine, you are the branches. He who abides in Me, and I in him,*
*bears much fruit; for without Me you can do nothing.*
John 15:5

I am a cluster, a full collection of grapes abiding in my Savior in the full
sunlight of His grace and wonder. It is a beautiful day, and the Master
comes to tend me.

He holds me tenderly in His hands, turning me to see how I am doing.
He gently snips some leaves away that are worn and have turned brown.
He then removes a leaf that is blocking the healing rays of His sun from
my life.

He is tending me for Himself, and He is very pleased with what He sees,
even though I haven't reached full maturity yet. As I rest in His hands,
no effort on my part, He will gently bring me to my maximum potential
of sweetness, fullness, and fruitfulness.

What Jesus is whispering to my heart today:

_____

_____

_____

_____

_____

# April 28

I spent many years sabotaging my walk with Jesus. I mean really. I really did that...

*For he who sows to his flesh will of the flesh reap corruption, but he who sows to the Spirit will of the Spirit reap everlasting life.*
Galatians 6:8

I would start my day meeting with Him in the morning, then spend the next 23.5 hours – when not sleeping – thinking about what the world thinks about, reading what the world reads, and viewing what the world views.

May I please say this plain and simple?

We don't have a lot of time here to waste on stupid stuff. I remember when my daughter was a newborn, and it seems like yesterday. My words are not to induce a guilt trip; neither are they an urging to try harder. Nevertheless, they are an invitation to pay attention to what we are paying attention to. It's that simple. Because what we are pursuing either leads to a dead-end or life in the power of the Holy Spirit.

And I be wanting me some of that power in the Spirit stuff!

What Jesus is whispering to my heart today:

_____

_____

_____

_____

_____

# April 29

When Jesus is all that I see – that I choose to see – from the first morning alarm to the final good-night kiss, life is different...

We all have received difficult, life-altering news at one time or another. And the trend for living in this broken, sin-scarred world is – there may be a good chance we will, at some time, face difficulty again. Now for the good news...

*I have set the LORD always before me;*
*Because He is at my right hand I shall not be moved.*
Psalm 16:8

When I cause Him to be all that fills and satisfies me, His presence encompasses my being just as *Psalm 139* shares. When I invite His Spirit to saturate my soul, and I feast on His Word, trials just don't have the effect they used to. I am no longer overcome, overwhelmed, undone, or shaken.

This is not the theory of Christianity, but the living, tangible reality of it and the irresistible truth of it. When I set the steady gaze of my heart and affections ever and only upon Him, He is all that I need. I am changed, and He will take care of the rest.

What Jesus is whispering to my heart today:

_____

_____

_____

_____

_____

# April 30

Moses hears these words. In the dirt and dust, he stands on holy ground.

*And God said to Moses, "I AM WHO I AM." And He said, "Thus you shall say to the children of Israel, 'I AM has sent me to you.'"*
Exodus 3:14

*Who should I say is sending me?* This is the question Moses asks of God. The reply? *I AM is sending you...*

*I AM.* God's Name that means simply *TO BE.* Think about it! Our God · is eternal, no beginning, no end. Not created; HE IS. He is outside of time, outside of human understanding, and out of the box. The *Uncaused Cause* – my Bible notes tell me. And then I read...

*Jesus said to them, "Most assuredly, I say to you, before Abraham was, I AM."* John 8:58

Here, Jesus establishes His divinity: co-equal, co-divine, co-eternal, and co-existent with the Father and the Holy Spirit. And so I remember. Yes, Jesus is my dearest friend, but He is the great I AM. I must never forget this because there are times when I am too casual, too cocky, or too something. When He invites me to dine with Him *Rev. 3:20,* I need to remember to come humbly and that I, like Moses, stand on holy ground.

What Jesus is whispering to my heart today:

_____

_____

_____

_____

_____

# May 1

I am plowing through the Book of Proverbs right now. Really.

These Proverbs. Well. They are just too cool. Just too something. Hmmmm, I know. They are very, very real, and they are very, very practical. No-brainers, really, except the Lord knows we need all the help we can get.

These Proverbs help us live life less chaotic and with less conflict, resulting in good choices and outstanding outcomes. Simple words to save us from heartache, torment, rabbit trails, and chasing the wind.

*Keep your heart with all diligence,*
*For out of it spring the issues of life.*
Proverbs 4:23

We need to guard our hearts for the Lord Jesus alone. Not looking to another - such as a husband, wife, friend - to fulfill something within us that only God Himself can give. This verse has brought immeasurable happiness to my marriage and all of my relationships! And, this is just one proverb.

So, get crackin'. There are thirty-one chapters filled with these nuggets: one each day for the next thirty-one days. Start finding treasures to add to your life's gems. You will be glad you did.

What Jesus is whispering to my heart today:

_____

_____

_____

_____

_____

# May 2

In the midst of this week…

Should life – aka the world, the flesh, and our enemy – throw you a curveball, well, you are already on the winning team in Christ. Let Him be your *catcher*. In other words, don't noodle, worry, be distracted, or become anxious about your situation. Place your concerns completely in His capable hands and let Him coach you about what to do next.
*Romans 8:37*

Should you grow impatient, weary, or wary, keep your eyes on King Jesus. Head to His throne room on your knees. Let the Holy Spirit fill you up and overwhelm you. His strength is all that you need.
*Hebrews 4:16*

This is a week of new beginnings, hopes to be realized, and miracles to watch for. Keep your eyes open, your heart tender, and your mind from distraction. This week will be awesome in Jesus because He Who is in you is greater than anything!
*1 John 4:4*

What Jesus is whispering to my heart today:

_____

_____

_____

_____

_____

# May 3

Are you like me, thirsty for His presence?

*O God, You are my God; Early will I seek You;*
*My soul thirsts for You; My flesh longs for You*
*In a dry and thirsty land where there is no water.*
Psalm 63:1

Yet, stuff is pressing. You know, the stuff of life: kids to race after, work deadlines to meet, cars to fix, sports to watch, and social media!!

A friend once likened our hunger and thirst for God to going grocery shopping. Yes. Really. It is dangerous to enter a market hungry. We tend to settle for the unhealthy stuff. The bag of chips looks more appetizing than the piece of fruit. Candy bars tantalize instead of whole grains. You get the drift. We settle for junk to satisfy instead of a luscious feast that would not only fill us, but nourish us and give us strength.

*Because Your lovingkindness is better than life…*
*My soul shall be satisfied as with marrow and fatness.*  Psalm 63:3-5

I have wasted too much time on the empty calories of the world. I want a meal. *The meal* with Jesus that He continually invites me to. Yes, I want to feast in His presence.

What Jesus is whispering to my heart today:

_____

_____

_____

_____

_____

# May 8

I lived several years when life seemed like a lot of toil without any return...

*When He had stopped speaking, He said to Simon, "Launch out into the deep and let down your nets for a catch." But Simon answered and said to Him, "Master, we have toiled all night and caught nothing; nevertheless at Your word I will let down the net.*
Luke 5:4-5

During those years, the Lord was doing something deep in me, and I am so grateful He did not give me what I thought I wanted at that time. I would have missed intimacy with Him completely. But now, He has spoken His word, and I have let down my net for the catch.

There is much to be said about His timing, and there is much to be said about just sitting in the boat with Jesus alone. Those times when we go so far out into the deep with God, there is no point of return to the things of this world. I think that was what those early years in my life were all about.

If you are in a period of waiting for the Lord to _____ (you fill in the blank) – take heart. Don't look down. Instead, look up. Don't hug the shore; go out further into the deep with Jesus and sit alone with Him in the boat for a while. Let Him do something eternal in your heart first, then when it is time for Him to speak His word to your situation, watch what happens.

What Jesus is whispering to my heart today:

_____

_____

_____

# May 9

In the midst of this week…

Should you be tempted to be discouraged about an aspect of your life, the same Holy Spirit, who raised Jesus from the dead, resides in *you*! Take time to drink deeply from His limitless well and be refreshed.
*Eph. 1:19-20*

Should you need to know God's will for your life, remember that He wants to make His plans known to you. Nevertheless, He often reveals only one step at a time and not the whole enchilada! He wants us to trust and listen for His voice daily. The dividends can be amazing. Remember? He gave His first disciples specific instructions to go back to Jerusalem. They obeyed, and through the power of encountering the Holy Spirit there, the world was forever changed!
*Colossians 1:9, Acts 2:1*

This is a week of new beginnings, hopes to be realized, and miracles to watch for. Keep your eyes open, your heart tender, and your mind from distraction. This week will be awesome in Jesus because He Who is in you is greater than anything!
*1 John 4:4*

.

What Jesus is whispering to my heart today:

_____

_____

_____

_____

_____

# May 10

All for joy...

*...looking unto Jesus, the author and finisher of our faith, who for the joy that was set before Him endured the cross, despising the shame, and has sat down at the right hand of the throne of God.*
Hebrews 12:2

King Jesus – fully God, co-equal, co-divine, co-eternal, and co-existent – endured the cross so many years ago for us. And yet…

King Jesus – was fully man. Simply read about the physical attributes of being crucified to realize somewhat what He went through for us. And yet…

It was the separation from the Father, as Abba-Daddy had to turn His gaze from the One so laden with our iniquity. That rending of the very fabric of Pure Love between the Father, the Son, and the Holy Spirit was the most horrendous torture He experienced for us.
And yet…

He did it all for joy. The joy of bringing us back home.

*But as many as received Him, to them He gave the right to become children of God, to those who believe in His name.* John 1:12

What Jesus is whispering to my heart today:

_____

_____

_____

_____

# May 11

Anybody feeling just a little overwhelmed right now?

*From the end of the earth I will cry to You,*
*When my heart is overwhelmed;*
*Lead me to the rock that is higher than I.*
Psalm 61:2

Too much stuff to do and too little time to do it? So many dreams, but not enough money to accomplish them? Join the club. I think most of humanity is feeling a little overwhelmed.

Nevertheless, King David tells us what to do and Who to look to for help. It is that simple. *Cry out!* He tells us. Cry out to your heavenly Father, who loves you beyond reason. Go to your room and pour out your heart. Lay it all out before Him. Then wait for His response.

Wait for the Holy Spirit to lift your gaze, your heart, and your spirit to *THE ROCK* – the Rock of Ages. Jesus hasn't moved, been shaken, or ever wavered. And, as He bends down to take you by the hand, look up as He draws you to Himself in safety on *His* higher ground.

And find rest, peace, and direction for your soul, for your life.

What Jesus is whispering to my heart today:

_____
_____
_____
_____
_____

# May 12

I am *pooped out*. However, it is a rich, good, joyous *pooped out!*

*But those who wait on the LORD Shall renew their strength;*
*They shall mount up with wings like eagles,*
*They shall run and not be weary,*
*They shall walk and not faint.*
Isaiah 40:31

I had the incredible privilege of sharing at a Women's Camp this past weekend. It was thrilling, it was exhilarating, and it was crazy-fun to watch the Lord at work. I could have talked about baking chocolate chip cookies, and He would have moved – transforming lives. His vast love for so many, going deep. Yes, going deep. He didn't need me.

I have lived too many years in the *other kind* of pooped out. You know, the burned out, exhausted, depleted, hope-dimmed, weary-of-life kind of pooped out. That type of living is *not* riding on eagles' wings. I don't want to live that way anymore.

Yet, the promise of soaring with Him is wrapped up in one word: *wait*. The kind of waiting that Mary did at His feet; drinking in His presence and His Word. That simple *Luke 10:38-42*. So, He calls me to *wait*. Yes, I am pooped out, but I am flying high!

What Jesus is whispering to my heart today:

_____

_____

_____

_____

_____

# May 13

Decisions are sometimes hard to make...

*Your ears shall hear a word behind you, saying,*
*"This is the way, walk in it," Whenever you turn to the right hand*
*Or whenever you turn to the left.*
Isaiah 30:21

Today, my elderly father decided to give up driving after eighty years on the road, and a young adult friend made a decision to go with chemo instead of a *wait-and-see* approach. Life-altering decisions.

My decisions today were tame in comparison. Where to eat? What to wear? What task to complete first? Yes, decisions, decisions. A day doesn't pass without a million choices for each of us, and we sure could use some help. Wouldn't you agree? Help from Someone with more perspective. Someone Who *knows* what's ahead. You know, Who knows what could happen. Someone who is *always* looking out for us.

Jesus is that Someone. However, He is a gentleman. He won't force His way where He is not invited or necessarily speak when we have already made our choice. He won't compete with the chatter of the world. But when we quiet our hearts and listen, giving Him full reign over our lives, we can be assured He will say, *This the way, walk in it.*

What Jesus is whispering to my heart today:

_____

_____

_____

_____

_____

# May 14

Sit on these phrases from *Psalm 63* for a while....

*Because Your lovingkindness is better than life.*

What has been ruling my *life*, robbing me of His lovingkindness and His unfailing love? Because whatever *it* is – that thing, person, circumstance, or passion of mine – can't compete with God's promise to satisfy my soul: my heart and mind, thoughts and emotions.

*I meditate on You in the night watches.*

What is consuming my thoughts? I need to take an honest inventory here. Are my thoughts leading me to Him, or are they the empty chatter of distraction? More harmful still, are my thoughts drawing me away from Jesus? I have a choice. And my joy, purpose, and *future* depend on what I am thinking about *now*.

*You have been my help,*
*Therefore in the shadow of Your wings I will rejoice.*

Yes, this is the place to be. My heart and mind tucked in close to His heart and mind. And when I follow right behind Him, the great promise of *Psalm 63* we have been reading is fulfilled: *His right Hand will uphold me.*

What Jesus is whispering to my heart today:

_____

_____

_____

_____

_____

# May 15

God could have created the world to be flat, square, octagonal, or any shape. His dimensions are not limited to merely three; they are limitless. Yet, He chose to make the world *round*.

*Through the LORD's mercies we are not consumed,*
*Because His compassions fail not.*
*They are new every morning;*
*Great is Your faithfulness.*
Lamentations 3:22-23

Every morning, every location on planet earth has the opportunity to start anew in Him. Yes, we can always call on Him any time of day to reach into our situations and breathe the freshness and newness of His power. Mornings, however, bring the promise of this truth, day after day after day.

Do you need a fresh start today? This is the day to rejoice in new beginnings! This is the day when He can take all of our past – good, bad, or ugly – and redeem it with His power and hope. He is there, just as He is each break of day, to move on your behalf. Simply ask for His help and get out of His glorious way.

What Jesus is whispering to my heart today:

_____

_____

_____

_____

_____

I am pretty sure Mary's gift was not only of great monetary cost, but also a sacrificed treasure of her heart…

*Then Mary took a pound of very costly oil of spikenard, anointed the feet of Jesus, and wiped His feet with her hair. And the house was filled with the fragrance of the oil.*
John 12:3

Maybe the oil was a cherished gift from Mary's parents. Possibly Mary paid for the aromatic oil with pennies she had long been saving, since she was but a wee one, for her wedding day. A treasure – hidden and tucked away. Maybe waiting for that special time when she could dab a little behind her ears. Possibly this oil was meant to last a lifetime.

This gift meant much to Mary, possibly with an attachment hidden deep within her emotions. Its outpouring was an act of greatest love, adoration, and sacrifice. If Mary chose to give something for the Saviour's benefit, she would offer it with all she had in her heart. And that is precisely what she did. Every. Last. Drop.

And the gift everyone received? The gift of an inescapable fragrance that filled the room. A fragrance that lingered long with those in its presence. Her simple gift was so profound that Mary's outpouring is recorded in the Bible. That is what a surrendered life does. It leaves an indelible impression on the lives it touches. I want that to be me, Lord.

What Jesus is whispering to my heart today:

_____

_____

_____

_____

# May 21

I love that my Bridegroom rejoices over me…

*For the LORD delights in you, And your land shall be married…*
*And as the bridegroom rejoices over the bride,*
*So shall your God rejoice over you.*
Isaiah 62:4b-5b

I have just been to too many weddings where the groom looked as if he was going to bust his buttons to get the ceremony over with and so he could run down the aisle with the woman of his dreams.

God is like that with us, even with our sins, stains, pettiness, and our stuff. He is still crazy about us. His Word tells us He even dances over every one of His cherished children.

The Lord's honeymoon with His beloved ones – you and me – is never over. He is just as passionate and fervent about each of us as He was the moment of our inception. His unfailing love has not failed toward you or me.

It might be time to remind yourself of this truth. How about stopping for a moment now and exchanging a few genuine heartfelt words with the One who loves us with such abandon. He is crazy about you and me.

What Jesus is whispering to my heart today:

_____

_____

_____

_____

_____

May 22

We have been given a sacred trust...

*Yet preaching the Good News is not something I can boast about. I am compelled by God to do it. How terrible for me if I didn't preach the Good News! But I have no choice, for God has given me this sacred trust.*
1 Corinthians 9:16-17 NLT

No, I am not comparing myself to Paul. Nevertheless, because Jesus lifted me from the *hot mess* of my life, I can't help but share! If *He* can do it for me, *He* can do it for anyone.

We have been given the *gift* of new life and the power to live that new life in Jesus. It is our *sacred trust*. Truthfully, I don't often think my sharing what I have in Christ in such terms, nevertheless a sacred trust is precisely what it is. So...

This week let's ask the Lord for the names of those we might start praying for and reaching out to within the circle of our influence. Someone we know needs Him, and we have a sacred trust to give away that they desperately need.

What Jesus is whispering to my heart today:

_____

_____

_____

_____

_____

# May 23

In the midst of this week...

Should your bank account go down, your blood pressure go up, or a loved one goes sideways on you, place your heart in His amazing Word. He has the final report. Enough said!
*Psalm 119:114*

Should you become over-scheduled, overwhelmed, or over-the-top nuts with stuff to do and no time to do it, take a breath, breathe a prayer, and be grateful for the One who came to give His all that we might live. For He alone is worthy and He has all your answers to slowing down the steam-roller of your life.
*Matthew 6:25-26*

This is a week of new beginnings, hopes to be realized, and miracles to watch for. Keep your eyes open, your heart tender, and your mind from distraction. This week will be awesome in Jesus because He Who is in you is greater than anything!
*1 John 4:4*

What Jesus is whispering to my heart today:

_____

_____

_____

_____

_____

# May 24

It might be time again to have a little *forgiveness* check-up…

*For if you forgive men their trespasses, your heavenly Father will also forgive you. But if you do not forgive men their trespasses, neither will your Father forgive your trespasses.*
Matthew 6:14-15

These are pretty heavy words from the mouth of our Savior – to completely forgive every person who has wounded, hurt, or abused us. However, I want to direct your attention to a different area of not being able to forgive.

Is there someone reading this who needs to forgive the Lord?

This happens, you know. Years ago, I felt this way about Him, but He met me in my need, hurt, and anger. He wasn't afraid to hear me out. It was when I tried to withhold my feelings from Him that I suffered. When I was ready to invite Him in to deal with this, He came.

Don't stomp off and be mad, sulk, or give up your faith. What good would that do? Run into His arms and talk to Jesus honestly and genuinely listen. Rely upon His unfailing Word and find comfort in His presence. Take it from one who knows.

What Jesus is whispering to my heart today:

_____

_____

_____

_____

_____

# May 25

I recently heard a Christian lament that our western culture sure can cause our following Jesus to be difficult at times.

*...and you are complete in Him, who is the head of all principality and power.*
Colossians 2:10

My friend was thinking of the trends, the sparkly toys, the relationships, and social media that constantly tempts us to believe would make life more satisfying, whole, and complete. She thought it might be easier to live in a third-world country without temptation. Not!

*I lived years* in dissatisfaction, partial living, and feeling oh so lacking. Believe me. It doesn't matter where you live. It is about the heart and the *felt presence* of the Holy Spirit.

A heart lost in Jesus' love *will* be satisfied, more than satisfied. A life in the power of the Spirit *will* ever be coming into greater wholeness, more than ever thought possible. We can experience a life so fulfilled in His extraordinary presence that we will love others freely without expectation. And, comparison with others loses its grip.

When filled with Christ, worldly sparkle starts to fizzle. Trends may come and go, but they will not shake us. I am just beginning to find this out for myself – right now, right where I live. You can, too.

What Jesus is whispering to my heart today:

_____

_____

_____

_____

# May 26

Have you ever made a bad decision that rocked your world?

*For He commands and raises the stormy wind,*
*Which lifts up the waves of the sea.*
*They mount up…They go down…*
*Their soul melts because of trouble.*

Many years ago, my husband and I made a really poor decision, not based on God's leading but due to our need. We, who would hope to lead folks in faith, were unwilling to live by faith. We lost just about everything.

*Then they cry out to the LORD in their trouble,*
*And He brings them out of their distresses.*

I do believe God sometimes ministers to us in a manner what some would call *a severe mercy*. We don't like the sound of those words; however, let me tell you: His *severe mercy* saved our lives. So, if you should be in a similar situation, bury your head and your heart into Jesus. Confess. Repent. Humble yourself. He will bring you to shore.

*He calms the storm, So that its waves are still…*
*So He guides them to their desired haven.*
Psalm 107:25-31

What Jesus is whispering to my heart today:

_____

_____

_____

_____

# May 27

While sitting in a large airport this afternoon I had a chance to observe...

*Are not two sparrows sold for a copper coin?*
*And not one of them falls to the ground apart from your Father's will.*
*But the very hairs of your head are all numbered.*
*Do not fear therefore; you are of more value than many sparrows.*
Matthew 10:29-31

I didn't used to like large groups of people, but – ahhh – freedom in Jesus. However, that is another story...

Today, I realized that I have a *thing* for airports. Amazing. I saw all different kinds of people – young, and old, trim and not so trim, and probably every color, tribe, and nation represented.

What are their stories? Where are they going and why? Is it for happy causes? Tragic reasons? Are they excited to see loved ones or bearing a heartache so great that they can barely breathe?

Yet, Jesus knows. Yes. He knows each one, even if they don't know Him yet. Someone needs to remember: His eye is on the sparrow and He watches over you.

What Jesus is whispering to my heart today:

_____

_____

_____

_____

_____

# June 1

Do you feel like you have *stalled* on your Journey in Jesus? The victories over life, self, and circumstances are at a standstill? Where is God?

*...being confident of this very thing, that He who has begun a good work in you will complete it until the day of Jesus Christ;*
Philippians 1:6

Don't worry about trying harder, being better, or getting your act together. You haven't been able to so far so why keep beating your head against the wall? It is time to let Him do the heavy lifting; the stuff you can't change about yourself or your circumstances. There is just one prerequisite...

Run to His presence. Do what you need to: confess, surrender, let go to Him, quit trying. Be willing to change any and everything, but don't attempt this without His presence and the power of His Word to speak fresh direction to your soul and spirit. Linger. Don't leave until the burdens start to lift – we tend to leave oh-too-early. Wait. Linger some more. Be refreshed *Isaiah 40:31*. Tomorrow, repeat. Then the next day, repeat again. And, so on. You won't be disappointed.

He is not finished with you yet. You can count on it.


What Jesus is whispering to my heart today:

_____

_____

_____

_____

_____

# June 2

If I could raise my children all over again...

*You will show me the path of life; In Your presence is fullness of joy; At Your right hand are pleasures forevermore.*
Psalms 16:11

Not that I didn't love and enjoy our three dear, beautiful, smart, fun, and crazy kids, but my brokenness and selfishness kept me from all the riches we could have had in Christ when they were young. Yet, I thank God for His love which progressively moved in my life, so that each subsequent child had a healthier and more-free mom than the one before them.

Still, with a *do-over,* I would make His presence the priority of my life and His fullness my daily purpose. I would choose to walk in His joy and happiness. And, I wouldn't worry about *teaching* my kids so much about Jesus; rather, they would *experience* Him through my life.

So, don't worry about being the perfect Christian parent. Instead, pursue Jesus till His presence runs through your veins, lights up your mind, and heals the deep recesses of your heart. Let His love rule your life and touch your kids. He will take care of the rest!

What Jesus is whispering to my heart today:

_____

_____

_____

_____

_____

# June 3

There is something about watching a river that is mesmerizing, refreshing, calming, yet exhilarating, all at the same time...

*... And You give them drink from the river of Your pleasures.*
Psalms 36:8

God calls us to drink deeply from His River, the third Person of the Trinity – the Holy Spirit *John 7:39*. And what a river He is. Ever in motion, removing obstacles, surmounting circumstances, and quenching thirsty souls. He is the beverage of life, pure delight, and extreme pleasure. His healing waters extend to anyone who will ask.

The Holy Spirit never stops moving on our behalf. Even when we sleep, turn away, or leave the River altogether, He never stops his forward motion. The Spirit of the Living God never stops, no matter what our state of mind or heart. He is there.

Needing some refreshment just now? Simply ask for His presence and His help. He promises to come, *Luke 11:13*. He will refresh, renew, and quench your thirst. So dive in and drink deeply.

What Jesus is whispering to my heart today:

---

---

---

---

---

# June 4

I am the first one to admit that I do not like change very much...

*But new wine must be put into new wineskins, and both are preserved.*
Luke 5:38

God is all about change. He is all about creativity. He is the One who flung the stars into the heavens like so much loose glitter, birthed each of us, no two alike, and orchestrates the individual movement of each ocean wave. Yes, the Lord is always up to something new.

I cannot take for granted how He will mastermind His work in my life. And, I cannot assume or presume that if He worked one way at one time, He would do the same thing the next time.

New wine is the *power of Pentecost*, the power of the Holy Spirit. If I am going to be a new wineskin that the Holy Spirit can use to minister His love and healing to people, I have to be open to His creativity at all times. Yes, I can and should stand on God's Word, but I must always remember that His Living Word, the Lord Jesus *John 1:14*, usually does not do the same thing twice.

In other words, be open for the Lord Jesus to surprise you!

What Jesus is whispering to my heart today:

_____

_____

_____

_____

_____

# June 5

I just don't think we get how much God loves us...

*He brought me to the banqueting house,*
*And his banner over me was love.*
Song of Songs 2:4

His banner, His heartbeat, His passion is *us*. He never speaks anything over our lives that isn't driven by pure, unfailing, powerful *agape* – all the time and unrelenting. There is nothing we can do to stop it love.

His banner over each and every one of us is love. He doesn't tell us: *you loser* or *worthless child.* These phrases are what the devil would whisper in our ears and we would believe and agree with.

Nope. I am not doing it anymore. Not agreeing with those lies. I just spent a wonderful day, here in Taiwan, with women from all over the world. We *chose* to believe and agree with His Word – *King Jesus' Word*. And that word is *LOVE.*

Yes. This is the truth. His truth that He bought and paid for by His precious blood. And the power of His Holy Spirit within me is more than enough. I choose to walk under His banner of love and it is beautiful.

What Jesus is whispering to my heart today:

_____
_____
_____
_____
_____

# June 6

In the midst of this week....

Should a situation in your life – financial, relational, physical – seem greater than what you can handle, He already knows. His strength is made perfect in your weakness!
*2 Cor. 12:9*

If a temptation overtakes you that you can't seem to find victory over, you may be dealing with a stronghold in your life. In other words, the adversary has taken some ground in an area of your soul – your heart and/or mind. Seek someone you can confess and be accountable to, and don't give up. Where the Spirit of the Lord is there is freedom!
*2 Cor. 3:17*

This is a week of new beginnings, hopes to be realized, and miracles to watch for. Keep your eyes open, your heart tender, and your mind from distraction. This week will be awesome in Jesus because He Who is in you is greater than anything!
*1 John 4:4*

What Jesus is whispering to my heart today:

_____

_____

_____

_____

_____

# June 7

Jesus gently draws us into this promise and draws us to Himself, *knowing* we will fall head over heels in love with Him...

*Delight yourself also in the LORD,*
*And He shall give you the desires of your heart.*
Psalm 37:4

He does this because He knows the things, people, positions, all that we think we desire can often be so far less than His plans for us.

In our broken state, we would often never even dream *His* dreams for us. He has an over-the-top, beyond-reason destiny for us to experience and fulfill. And yet, through the messed-up lens of our lives before His transforming work, the desires of our heart are often so miserably pitiful compared to what He has in store.

For instance, a person has to be set free from fear and insecurity before dreaming big dreams. Someone needs to become safe in His love before they will dare to love with abandon. One needs liberty from the oppression of guilt before they can raise their head to walk in all that the Holy Spirit has. You get the idea. So, *fall* for Him. His desires for you are so far beyond what you could imagine or think *Isaiah 64:4*.

What Jesus is whispering to my heart today:

_____

_____

_____

_____

_____

# June 8

We have been created in God's image, so each and every one of us has a creative bent...

*In the beginning God created the heavens and the earth.*
Genesis 1:1

You know, something we like to do, something we make, or something we form. Yes, something we create. Something which brings us pleasure.

For years, I literally sewed all of our family's clothing. I became pretty good at it and could even design a little bit. I liked crafts. You name it, I tried it. I loved to cook, trying new recipes and creating new ones. However, with my schedule now, all of those things have flown the coop. Honestly, I have no desire to pick them up again. Now, I write.

Notice, I don't say I *write well*. It didn't take long for me to figure out I wasn't the next Max Lucado, Francis Chan, or Beth Moore! And I almost gave up on it because I didn't have a large audience. Why bother? But, I get such a kick out of it, and the Lord told me He does too, when I write.

What have you given up on or never tried because you thought *why bother*? I think our creative God created us in His image for *His* pleasure and *ours*. Let the joy begin.

What Jesus is whispering to my heart today:

_____

_____

_____

_____

_____

# June 9

On this Journey of Life, the Bible is the Jesus Follower's Guidebook...

*Your word is a lamp to my feet And a light to my path.*
Psalms 119:105

This amazing Book can tell us where the most beautiful sights are; what places to stay away from; how to interact with the locals; the best places to feast; and where to find refuge. Written by One who knows the journey and terrain like no one else and who knows *you* like no one else, the Word of God will make the difference between a horrible experience and the trip of a lifetime.

Yet, on our Journey of Life, most of us try to navigate its path on our own. We run out the door ill-prepared to live life to the fullest in the broken, messed-up world we live in. We need help. And fast.

Without consulting the Guidebook, we lose our footing, go where we shouldn't, take wrong turns, and get in trouble with people. Instead of a trip of wonder, joy, and promise, it is usually about survival and how to make it through another day. Often, we have no clue where we are or any idea of how to get to the final destination. Need I say more?

We only have one life to live. Let's live it in the light of God's Word.

What Jesus is whispering to my heart today:

_____

_____

_____

_____

_____

# June 10

At this moment, does your life feel, look, or seem like a roller coaster?

*For He is the living God, And steadfast forever; His kingdom is the one which shall not be destroyed, And His dominion shall endure to the end.* Daniel 6:26

When my husband and I first took the pastorate of the church we are currently at, the small band of folks were meeting for services in a hotel right next to a large, northern California amusement park. In prayer one Sunday morning, I looked out and saw the crazy, anxiety-driven rides across the street and thought they sure looked like our lives at the time.

Nevertheless, in an instant, I sensed the Lord Jesus showing me a *straight line,* gently increasing upward above the ins-and-outs and the ups-and-downs of the roller coaster. He was telling me to keep my eyes fully on His steadfastness and not the crazy twists and turns of my life.

Whatever you are facing, the Lord is with you. *Look up.* Secure your heart on His proven word – it is the steadfast line above the wild ride. However, you need to keep a light touch on *how* or *when* He works on your behalf. Keep a confident heart in Him who is greater than the roller coaster you are on. He still delivers and rescues, just as Daniel knew. He still works signs and wonders.

What Jesus is whispering to my heart today:

_____

_____

_____

_____

_____

# June 11

A longtime friend once told me I had given some great advice...

*To the Chief Musician. A Psalm of David the servant of the LORD...*
Psalms 18:1a

This is what she credits me for saying...

*The Book of Psalms in the Bible is like a medicine cabinet. Whatever you are experiencing, simply open up the Psalms and you will find exactly what you need to help you.*

Truly I don't remember saying this. *Nevertheless*, whoever said it to her, well, it *is* the truth.

- ☆ Are you discouraged? Open the Psalms
- ☆ Are you sick in heart or body? Open the Psalms
- ☆ Are you frustrated? Open the Psalms
- ☆ Are you giddy with joy and feel like dancing? Open the Psalms
- ☆ Are grateful for your wonderful King? Open the Psalms

So here is your prescription: before you go to bed tonight, read two to three psalms, depending on your circumstances and condition. Drink a full cup of the Holy Spirit's living water with your dosage.

Sleep well. Repeat in the morning.


What Jesus is whispering to my heart today:

_____

_____

_____

_____

_____

# June 12

Really. Every one of us is a *leader*...

*From the clan of Hebron came Hashabiah. He and his relatives—1,700 capable men—were put in charge of the Israelite lands west of the Jordan River. They were responsible for all matters related to the things of the LORD and the service of the king in that area.*
1 Chronicles 26:30

We *are* all called, and all Christ-followers have the Holy Spirit residing in them. All of us can pass on what we know and love about Jesus and His Word to another. You have something that someone else needs. You have *Someone* that someone else needs, too. Don't let others have all the fun and excitement. Really.

Starbuck's is just waiting for you to reach out to your co-worker, neighbor, or friend, and show up for an informal time of studying God's Word together. You might try using the simple CrossPointe Bible Study tools that can be found online at Amazon.com. Or simply meet to talk about life together in Him. There is someone *waiting* for you.

And, *you are* a leader.

What Jesus is whispering to my heart today:

_____
_____
_____
_____
_____

# June 13

In the midst of this week...

If your kids are whining, your workmates are irritating, and the neighbors won't mow their lawn, it is probably a sign your soul is running on empty! It is time to get filled up, saturated, and doused in the Holy Spirit. Get alone with the Lord and His Word, rest in His presence, and get fueled up to greet the week ahead.
*Psalm 16:11*

If you are feeling burnt out, stressed out, or wiped out – again, it is time to return to the living waters of the Holy Spirit. Are you unsure about His work in you? It is time to spend some time getting to know Who He is. Take a look at the Gospel of *John, Chapters 14, 15,* and *16.* Don't remain a desert when you can become an oasis.

This is a week of new beginnings, hopes to be realized, and miracles to watch for. Keep your eyes open, your heart tender, and your mind from distraction. This week will be awesome in Jesus because He Who is in you is greater than anything!
*1 John 4:4*

What Jesus is whispering to my heart today:

_____

_____

_____

_____

_____

# June 14

What has come your way in the past few days or weeks?

*Let us therefore come boldly to the throne of grace,*
*that we may obtain mercy and find grace to help in time of need.*
Hebrews 4:15-16

I am continually reminded of this passage and the invitation the Word of God presents to us to come to Him with *all* things, every *trial* and *temptation*. And the invite? To come boldly, freely, and with fearless confidence, cheerful courage, and assurance. And, the location of the invite? God's very throne room.

Sometimes, I seem to think it is more comforting to call a friend first for aid or let the enemy lull me into a sense of self-pity. I may call a *prayer warrior* I know to do the heavy-lifting before the Lord. But, no...

*I* am the one invited to a front row seat, coming humbly, yet boldly, into my Savior's courts. And the promise? His beyond-reason grace, His matchless mercy, and His infinite help to do the impossible.

So, whomever you might contact initially with a current crisis, instead, call, come to, and linger at the foot of the Lord Jesus' throne, first.

What Jesus is whispering to my heart today:

_____

_____

_____

_____

_____

# June 15

I get distracted so easily, do you?

*...praying always with all prayer and supplication in the Spirit, being watchful to this end with all perseverance and supplication for all the saints.*
Ephesians 6:18

I want each day to count for Christ. Indeed, He has blessed me with a wonderful *marketplace ministry* of speaking into, praying with, and encouraging the lives of many of my co-workers. Still...

I find my heart wanting to stay focused on interceding for others – not always my *strong suit*. The Holy Spirit knows I need a *lot* of help. He dropped into my heart that I should get a little journal. Now, every morning during a quiet time with Him, He gives me that day's prayer assignment with an accompanying verse to record in my little book.

I still get distracted, however, so I usually only list a few folks or circumstances a day and this little journal keeps me focused. Best of all, I have a record for the answers to prayers when they are fulfilled.

The moral of this story? I believe prayer is the battlefield where we take back ground the enemy has stolen from our lives and the lives of others. We need to be intentional, lest we be distracted. *Just sayin'*.

What Jesus is whispering to my heart today:

_____

_____

_____

_____

# June 16

Ask those who know me well what my dream job would be...

*Commit your way to the LORD,*
*Trust also in Him, And He shall bring it to pass.*
Psalm 37:5

I am in an airport again, watching the folks on the tarmac with the orange light batons escorting planes either home or to catch the air currents. And yes. That would be my dream job. Nevertheless, God has other plans.

For the last several years I have done a lot of one-on-one ministry. I often get to see someone coming home to salvation in Christ. Often, I get to watch the Holy Spirit cause someone's wings to soar in all He has for them as old strongholds or bondages are broken by His extravagant grace and power.

This weekend, a team of ladies and I are going to see the Lord move in setting free a good-sized number of women. This has been a dream of mine and I would love your prayers for this Steps to Breakthrough Conference. I don't know all that I will get to see Him do, but I am ready with my *orange lights*. So...

He sees your dreams too. Let Him fulfill them His way. And let me tell you, His way is so much better than anything we could choose.

What Jesus is whispering to my heart today:

_____

_____

_____

_____

# June 17

His presence is always *present*.

*God our refuge and strength.*
*A very present help in trouble.*
*Therefore we shall not fear…*
Psalm 46:1-2a

Some years ago, I decided I wouldn't live another day without His presence. Come hell or high water, I choose to nurture, not only a devotional time with Jesus – praying requests, reading the Word, journaling – but a frequent waiting and basking in the Holy Spirit who reveals the Savior within us and to us *John 16*.

Believe me, my family and the church we pastor have experienced some *crazy* stuff during these years, yet His presence has *always* been present. I can tell you story after ridiculously loving story of Jesus in our midst.

Now, what used to be mere theory has become reality. He is the real deal and He wants you to draw close and really *know* Him, not just know *about* Him. His present presence is all you need.

What Jesus is whispering to my heart today:

_____

_____

_____

_____

_____

# June 18

A woman became really upset with me a couple of years ago…

*Not that we are sufficient of ourselves to think of anything as being from ourselves, but our sufficiency is from God,*
2 Corinthians 3:5

The woman was peeved when I told her that her own ability to be self-sufficient was probably her biggest hindrance in following Christ. She didn't like that and she was very proud of her accomplishments, except for the fact she was losing her family.

Some of us facing trials truly believe we can pull ourselves through in our own strength. We have a bounty of God-given natural ability, just like the woman above. Others of us know we can't do anything to help ourselves, so we rely on others rather than the All Sufficient One.

No matter what camp you fall into: self-reliant or others-reliant, it is time to walk onto level ground found at the foot of His cross.

What Jesus is whispering to my heart today:

_____

_____

_____

_____

_____

# June 19

I don't think knowing God's will for your life is rocket science.

*Don't copy the behavior and customs of this world, but let God transform you into a new person by changing the way you think. Then you will learn to know God's will for you, which is good and pleasing and perfect.* Romans 12:2 NLT

To know God's personal adventure for you – the word *plan* here is simply way too tame – you and I need to have a paradigm shift in the way we think. Yes, a complete overhaul.

I didn't have a clue how much the world influenced the way I thought and it still can often have a pretty good grip on me. However, the wind of the Holy Spirit began blowing some cobwebs – some chains – away. Only He could do that.

The shift in my thinking came when I didn't just read the Bible to learn more, but when I also lapped up His word with the intent of hearing what He had to say to me personally. I started to know and recognize His voice, His heart, His way of doing things, and His will for me.

Nope. Not rocket science. It is simply having my thoughts and life transformed by the Master Creator.

What Jesus is whispering to my heart today:

_____

_____

_____

_____

_____

# June 20

In the midst of this week…

Should you receive some difficult news about a loved one, you are not defenseless. You have the Holy Spirit living inside of you and it is time to lean into the Commander of Heaven's Hosts. Pray what you know, pray what you sense He is telling you, and pray in the Spirit. You have the resources of heaven working on your loved one's behalf. Then stand firm and trust.
*2 Corinthians 10:4*

Should you feel confused about an area of your life, beat it back to God's Word. Run back to the last thing the Lord spoke to your heart about this situation. The enemy is probably trying to distract you. Enough said.
*1 Corinthians 14:33*

This is a week of new beginnings, hopes to be realized, and miracles to watch for. Keep your eyes open, your heart tender, and your mind from distraction. This week will be awesome in Jesus because He Who is in you is greater than anything!
*1 John 4:4*

What Jesus is whispering to my heart today:

_____

_____

_____

_____

_____

# June 21

The Lord *is* a strong tower *and* a stronghold for us...

*The LORD is good, A stronghold in the day of trouble; And He knows those who trust in Him.*
Nahum 1:7

*The name of the LORD is a strong tower; The righteous run to it and are safe.* Proverbs 18:10

We can hide in His safety no matter what the world or the devil is throwing at us. Still, there is ever so much a piece of the equation that involves our heart, and our heart is the only thing that truly matters.

Jesus is our stronghold in the day of trouble, yet we must *trust Him completely* to experience this truth. Eeeeeek!! We may *say* all the right things, yet are we genuinely putting the total weight of our trust and expectancy upon Him? Are we putting the full load of our worry in His hands and *letting go of the outcomes we desire*?

To be hidden in the strong tower and refuge of *His* glorious name, our hearts must run with complete abandon to Him. This isn't a casual *mosey*-along the path walk. Instead, it is desperation for His presence and His will alone, no matter what we face. Because our God will not fail.

What Jesus is whispering to my heart today:

_____

_____

_____

_____

_____

# June 22

There is such great comfort and strength from Jesus' words...

*Heaven and earth will pass away,*
*but My words will by no means pass away.*
Matthew 24:35

In the whole of this passage, Jesus is telling us about the end times of Planet Earth. However, *His Word* will not pass away, cannot be destroyed, cannot fade, whither, lose strength, power, or purpose.

How much time and effort I spend in and on things that are so temporary! So futile, oh so empty.

His Word is my strength, bread, breath, healer, corrector, teacher, and guidance counselor. His Word is everything. When we open its pages, the Holy Spirit reveals Jesus, Who is the Living Word; breathing His life-breath into our souls. What treasure! *John 1:14*

Nope. I don't want to waste time chasing the winds of futility any longer.

What Jesus is whispering to my heart today:

_____

_____

_____

_____

_____

# June 23

Jesus takes so *little* and makes *so much…*

*So they all ate and were filled. And they took up twelve baskets full of fragments and of the fish.*
Mark 6:42-43

Where do we feel small and insufficient? Is it our lives, our resources, our future – ourselves? Like the bread in His hands, He may need to *break* some things up in us to bring multiplication. Yet, there is no fear in His tender touch.

I love knowing everyone was *filled*. I spent so much of my life unsatisfied and frustrated. Ministry was more chore than overflow. The lack of knowing God's will for my life was the norm. And struggling with habitual behaviors almost destroyed me. Yet Jesus cornered me and I found that in *Him alone* I was satisfied, significant, and complete.

Lastly, Jesus doesn't *waste* anything. There isn't anything in our lives, even the months and years we regret, that He will not use for His glory. His grace not only extends to our present and our future, He causes everything to become part of our glorious story. No, nothing is wasted in Him. Truly.

How does this story speak to you? Why not take a few moments and talk to the Lord Jesus about it. He's ready to begin a miracle.

What Jesus is whispering to my heart today:

_____

_____

_____

_____

# June 24

My easy-going personality loves to be, well, easy-going…

*So it was, when Jesus returned…a woman, having a flow of blood for twelve years…came from behind and touched the border of His garment. And immediately her flow of blood stopped.*
Luke 8:40a, 43-44

However, there is a different kind of take-it-easy attitude that isn't restful, refreshing, or relaxing. This takes place when my relationship with Jesus becomes, well, easy-going or casual.

Been there, done that. I am through with this kind of walk in Jesus. It's more like drifting or coasting and it requires a lot more effort. Drifting takes its toll: unwanted worry, purposelessness, and just getting by, instead of glory, wonder, and realizing the supernatural in everyday life

This dear woman *pursued* the One and Only. She didn't care about the crowds, the time constraints, and the inconvenience. She wanted *Him*. The hem of His garment was more than enough. Nothing easy-going about her actions. And she was forever healed. Forever marked as His.

This isn't a guilt trip. It *is* His love's call to an over-the-top life in His wonder, presence, power, joy – versus – just casual, easy-as-you-please drifting. I've made my choice, Lord. Here I come.

What Jesus is whispering to my heart today:

_____

_____

_____

_____

_____

# June 25

As we press through these incredible seasons of upheaval in our world, perhaps it is time to drink the *I will* passages of God's Word.

*...I will strengthen you, Yes, I will help you, I will uphold you with My righteous right hand.*
Isaiah 41:10b

Are you tempted to be fearful, anxious, or discouraged, may I suggest that you turn to these passages and let the Holy Spirit breathe fresh faith into your soul. Take a look at *Exodus 6:6*-8 or *Isaiah 41:10-20*.

Underline in your Bible or Bible app how many times the Lord Almighty promises that He will come through for you. Meditate and yes, soak in His Word and presence until His peace restores your heart.

Certainly, we must and can encourage one another through these waves of uncertainty. Nevertheless, it is only the Lord Jesus' voice that can cut to the chase and reach our hearts with His comfort and promises by the Holy Spirit. His Word and His report are the only ones that matter. Really.

He is waiting for you to come to Him, and He is more than willing to grant His promises.

What Jesus is whispering to my heart today:

_____

_____

_____

_____

_____

# June 26

I, for one, really like shortcuts...

*Then Jesus returned in the power of the Spirit to Galilee, and news of*
*Him went out through all the surrounding region.*
Luke 4:14

Our Savior's ministry began with a temptation. His adversary, the devil, offered Jesus a *shortcut* to bypass the agony of the cross and take authority over the world. Jesus didn't buy into these lies, and neither should we.

Is there an area in our lives where taking a shortcut is more appealing than going God's route? Are we tempted with making a compromise that will satisfy us for a moment then leave us holding ashes?

I had just such an area today. Yet, I don't want to miss being transformed into God's image-bearer or knowing Jesus more dearly by cutting corners on His journey for me.

Nope. I'm settling in for the scenery of the possibly longer path. The Lord has never failed me, and I don't want to miss where He is taking me by settling for less. I desire the whole beautiful journey – I am saying goodbye to shortcuts!

What Jesus is whispering to my heart today:

_____

_____

_____

_____

_____

# June 27

In the midst of this week…

Don't lose the sense of His presence! Keep cultivating your time alone with Him and the Word of God. Keep pouring into others so that all will know Him. Keep sensitive to His leading – He has some stuff for you to do this week!
*Matthew 6:6*

On the other hand…

Should you be starting the week on a low note, a bland hope, a disabled joy; still follow the directions given above. Cultivate your time alone with the Lord of Heaven's Armies. Let His Word speak to your heart and heal your dimmed expectations by letting Him be your only expectation. He won't disappoint!
*Psalm 27:4*

This is a week of new beginnings, hopes to be realized, and miracles to watch for. Keep your eyes open, your heart tender, and your mind from distraction. This week will be awesome in Jesus because He Who is in you is greater than anything!
*1 John 4:4*

What Jesus is whispering to my heart today:

_____
_____
_____
_____
_____

# June 28

Sometimes you just have to read between the commas…

*…the eyes of your understanding being enlightened; that you may know what is the hope of His calling, what are the riches of the glory of His inheritance in the saints,*
Ephesians 1:18

The riches of the gospel of Jesus Christ are laid out for us in a few short words from Paul's prayer here, and these few words can change your life. Really.

Try it. Simply read the one verse above – savoring each phrase – between the *commas*. I believe the Lord has something to speak into your current situation from these three phrases. Ponder His words to you in this moment. What applies to you? How is your heart being moved or *wrecked* for His glory?

Let's slow down. Let's savor God's Word. Let's read between the commas, and be transformed.

What Jesus is whispering to my heart today:

_____

_____

_____

_____

_____

# June 29

Oh my. Going back to work, or school, or home after a week-long vacation is sometimes hard to do. Anybody know what I am talking about? And yet…

As Pastor Wayne Cordeiro would share, my position at my workplace, well, it is just my disguise. For instead of being an *Operations Specialist*, I am really, truly, on assignment for the King. Working in Administration for a large health care organization is really my *cover* for bringing Jesus wherever my foot falls.

*Walk in wisdom toward those who are outside*
*redeeming the time. Let your speech always be with grace…*
Colossians 4:5-6

So today, as we head to the place where we spend most of our time, let's let the Holy Spirit put a fresh spring in our step. Let Him put fresh vision in our hearts and fresh purpose for what we are really up to and about.

Let's bring heaven to earth with every footstep. And we can bet on it. Living under *His* assignment, rather than just for a paycheck, makes any position we may have crazy fulfilling.

What Jesus is whispering to my heart today:

_____

_____

_____

_____

_____

# June 30

Have you ever attempted to be close to someone, but they weren't interested? God has:

*I was sought by those who did not ask for Me; I was found by those who did not seek Me. I said, 'Here I am, here I am,' To a nation that was not called by My name. I have stretched out My hands all day long to a rebellious people...*
Isaiah 65:1-2a

He is speaking to Israel through these words, nevertheless, He is speaking to us as well...*here I am, here I am.*

Honestly, how many of us go through the day missing Him completely? Myself included. Yet, I am trying not to miss Him as much anymore. When He calls my name, when He reaches out, when He wants to meet at Starbuck's so-to-speak, I want to accept the invite. It is always a treat to spend time with Jesus.

I'm tired of Him always having to do the *work*. I want to seek Him, give Him a jingle throughout my day, and press into His presence. Somehow, I know He finds great delight in that – even from little ole' me. Yes, how about we all *surprise* the Lord and invite Him for a time of some sweet conversation and deeper relationship before our day is through?

What Jesus is whispering to my heart today:

_____

_____

_____

_____

_____

# July 1

Take a deep, long, slow drink of David's Shepherd Psalm 23 AMP:

*The Lord is my Shepherd [to feed, guide, and shield me], I shall not lack. He makes me lie down in [fresh, tender] green pastures; He leads me beside the still and restful waters.*

*He refreshes and restores my life (my self); He leads me in the paths of righteousness [uprightness and right standing with Him—not for my earning it, but] for His name's sake.*

*Yes, though I walk through the [deep, sunless] valley of the shadow of death, I will fear or dread no evil, for You are with me; Your rod [to protect] and Your staff [to guide], they comfort me.*

*You prepare a table before me in the presence of my enemies. You anoint my head with [a]oil; my [brimming] cup runs over.*

*Surely or only goodness, mercy, and unfailing love shall follow me all the days of my life, and through the length of my days the house of the Lord [and His presence] shall be my dwelling place."*

Life doesn't get any better than this and anything the world might offer doesn't even come close.

What Jesus is whispering to my heart today:

_____

_____

_____

_____

_____

July 2

If only. Sigh...

*He would have fed them also with the finest of wheat; And with honey from the rock I would have satisfied you.*
Psalms 81:16

These words come at the end of Psalm 81 and its author is lamenting – *if only*.

*If only* Israel had not been so stubborn-hearted and did only what they wanted to do or thought was best. *If only.*

Please tell me. Has being stubborn or insisting on our own way ever gotten us anywhere? Has doing what we wanted to do, no matter what He thinks, ever been satisfying?

Nope. No more *if only's* for me. Though I am far from perfect in my pursuit of God's all, I have tasted His honey from the rock and been wholly saturated and filled to the full with the wheat of His presence. I'm not going back to striving for my stubborn, less-than will.

Not in a million years.

What Jesus is whispering to my heart today:

_____

_____

_____

_____

_____

July 7

Has your week been crazy like mine?

*For thus says the Lord GOD, the Holy One of Israel: "In returning and rest you shall be saved; In quietness and confidence shall be your strength. But you would not...you said, "No, for we will flee on horses..."* Isaiah 30:15-16a

In the last few days, I have been just like the folks God was talking to in this passage. I have been in a hurry, trying to make my own way and trying to cram things into my life that Jesus had not called me to do! I started to let myself get distracted from *His presence*.

Only when I still my heart with Him, far from the maddening, crowded pace of life, does direction come. Only there do I experience overwhelming peace. Only there do I bubble with insatiable joy. Only there am I refreshed, restored, and renewed by the Holy Spirit.

So, I've come off of my *swift horse* and taken a few moments to *return* to Jesus and bask restfully in His tender and life-giving love and strength. Whew!  Life is so much sweeter and richer.

Do you need to do some *returning*?

What Jesus is whispering to my heart today:

_____

_____

_____

_____

_____

# July 8

I have long known this to be true about myself...

*O my soul, you have said to the LORD, "You are my Lord, My goodness
is nothing apart from You.*
Psalms 16:2

Yes, the Holy Spirit is working out His fruit of goodness in my life by
healing me of deep insecurities. And isn't most evil driven by insecurity?
Nevertheless, when it is time for me to breathe my last, there will still be
only *ONE* who is good.

I love the Amplified Version of this verse: *I say to the Lord, You are my
Lord; I have no good beside or beyond You.*

The *buck* stops with God. He stands alone in the *good* category. There
isn't any reason to look *beyond* Him for the inestimable, incomparable,
matchless goodness in life.

And yet, my wandering heart will try to look beyond. What folly.

Yes, God's goodness is enough – all I need. And my portion for walking
in His path? Life lived to the full, in His presence. His joy unspeakable
and full of glory, and His satisfying pleasure. Yes. He is good.

What Jesus is whispering to my heart today:

_____

_____

_____

_____

_____

# July 9

Circumstances are usually never what is *really* happening...

*Then the men of Israel took some of their provisions; but they did not ask counsel of the Lord.*
Joshua 9:14

When Joshua led the children of Israel into their Land of Promise, the Lord told him not to make any covenants or pledges with people they would displace as Israel removed nation after nation.

Out of nowhere, a bunch of rag-tag men appeared, claiming to be from a distant land. Their clothes were in tatters, their shoes were worn out, and of all things, they even had moldy bread. These guys lived just around the corner, the corner God had promised Joshua and his people. Oh, my goodness. *Israel did not ask the counsel of the Lord.*

I have been there too many times. Circumstances are seldom what they seem. We walk by faith and not by sight. The Bible clearly tells us that the unseen matters of the Spirit are far more the *real deal* than what we can see, taste, touch, smell, or hear.

So, let's be people who consult God about, well, everything. No, not necessarily what tube of toothpaste to buy, but just about everything else. Because there is a lot more going on than we can see. However, He sees it all.

What Jesus is whispering to my heart today:

_____

_____

_____

_____

# July 10

This has been my anthem for a few weeks now…

*Every morning*
   *you'll hear me at it again.*
*Every morning*
   *I lay out the pieces of my life*
   *on your altar*
   *and watch for fire to descend.*
Psalm 5:2-3 MSG

Maybe I'm just getting older, or maybe I'm feeling that I've wasted so much time in my Journey in Jesus. But honestly, I just want leave it all on the field. You know, the field of my life.

So lately, every morning, I lay the pieces of my life on His altar and watch for fire to descend. I want all the *me* stuff to burn away and let Jesus be all that is left. I have seen more crazy-sweet, powerful stuff happen in the last few days because of His in-filling.

Yes. I think this is going to be my prayer for a long, long time.

What Jesus is whispering to my heart today:

_____

_____

_____

_____

_____

# July 11

In the midst of this week...

Should the car not start, the kids or co-workers won't stop whining, the wallet seems empty, and the to-do list is overwhelming, look up! Remember, the Holy Spirit is with you in *everything* from the mundane to the life-altering. Hand everything over to His care for He can handle *everything*.
*Ephesians 1:19-20*

Should a relationship that seems oh so difficult right now in your home, work, school, or wherever, God is probably using it in your life – get this – to change and transform you. Don't worry about the other individual changing first; Jesus is wanting to do tender heart surgery in *you*.
*Proverbs 27:17*

This is a week of new beginnings, hopes to be realized, and miracles to watch for. Keep your eyes open, your heart tender, and your mind from distraction. This week will be awesome in Jesus because He Who is in you is greater than anything!
*1 John 4:4*

What Jesus is whispering to my heart today:

_____

_____

_____

_____

_____

July 12

It just takes some sunbathing in Honolulu to realize appearance doesn't matter. Really…

…For the LORD does not see as man sees;
for man looks at the outward appearance, but the LORD looks at the heart.
1Samuel 16:7

We love Hawaii. My husband loves to walk, but simply give me a beach chair, a ton of sunscreen, an iced tea and I am a happy camper. Yet, as I watch several thousand folks out on that white sand with Diamond Head in my frame, there is maybe one Perfect 10 out there. That man or woman, well, they are a rare group and I *ain't* in that group. Maybe you aren't either. Still, I am more than okay with that realization.

Just sayin' – Jesus looks at our hearts and if we let Him really heal our hearts; our negative thoughts about ourselves won't run our lives. Only He can do this. As someone set free years ago from a deeply entrenched eating disorder, I have found the joy of this truth. And, our bodies tend to follow His game plan of health when our hearts are healed. Go figure.

So whether, you are male or female, let Him have at your heart. You are a Perfect 10 in His eyes – let Him set you free to comprehend it, too.

What Jesus is whispering to my heart today:

_____
_____
_____
_____
_____

# July 13

What a great salvation we have…

*…how shall we escape if we neglect so great a salvation, which at the*
*first began to be spoken by the Lord, and was confirmed to us by those*
*who heard Him,*
Hebrews 2:3

How often I take this great salvation lightly that He suffered and
purchased for me when I choose to live a so-less-than life by
neglecting...

...to trust His grace to wholly forgiven me, and I give place to guilt.
...to lean hard into His comfort when needed, and I run to others first.
...to contend for physical healing; the healing He purchased for me.
...to take the authority over the adversary He has given me in His Name.
...to allow the Holy Spirit to manifest His power, gifts, and fruit in my
life.

I am learning, and I am learning slowly. But I am learning, hungering,
and desiring to live each moment in God's great salvation.

What Jesus is whispering to my heart today:

_____

_____

_____

_____

_____

# July 14

I just came from our grandson's first birthday celebration.

*Therefore, if anyone is in Christ, he is a new creation; old things have passed away; behold, all things have become new.*
2 Corinthians 5:17

I look into this little boy's adorable blue eyes and see the innocence, sweetness, and wonder he beholds. Everything about his life is new and fresh as each day dawns, and he awakens knowing he is loved and cherished beyond imagining.

Our life in Jesus can be like this, too. I used to think the daily wonder of experiencing Him was just for new believers, but the Holy Spirit has a way of breaking up those lies. Just read the *Book of Acts*. The past eleven years have been the best of my life and, like my little grandson, I can truly say, that I awaken each day expectant for the adventure the Lord will take me on next. Most of all, I am learning to be secure in my Father's love.

If your walk with Jesus has lost its innocence, sweetness, and wonder – you know, the fresh swell of excitement in the air – talk to Him about it. Ask for a fresh overflow of the Holy Spirit. Read the book of Acts again. Believe that these words are for you, because they are.

Let's begin to awaken with wonder again.

What Jesus is whispering to my heart today:

_____

_____

_____

_____

_____

July 15

Oceans. The song *Oceans* by Hillsong United was playing on my
Pandora channel today...

Hearing the song reminded me of deep waters in recent years. You know,
the usual: diagnosed with Stage 4 terminal cancer, son leaving the faith,
being laid off from work, to name a few events. Anyone understand?

And yet, the God of the Angel Armies was greater than anything I faced.
Those deep waters became training ground for walking in HIS power and
authority.

*Finally, my brethren, be strong in the Lord and in the power of His*
*might.* Ephesians 6:10

The Lord God turned each one of those situations around. Yes, He did it.
However, He also invited me to partner with Him in the battle by
standing in *His* power – *not* my worry, weakness, or wonderment, though
that was tempting to overtake me.

What is your *ocean* at the moment? Fill in the blank_____. Let's be
encouraged to put on God's armor for ourselves and see the enemy of
our souls be toppled in Jesus' Name. Are you ready for some water
walking?

What Jesus is whispering to my heart today:

_____

_____

_____

_____

_____

July 16

The Lord just gently nudged me. I have stopped looking for Him in the everyday moments of life and I've missed many of His love notes to me.

*But their eyes were restrained, so that they did not know Him.*
Luke 24:16

On the road to Emmaus, the two disciples did not recognize the Lord Jesus has He walked and talked with them. It seems so unbelievable that they could not have realized it was Him.

Yet that is what I have been doing this last several weeks. Not asking for my eyes to be opened all the time to see Him everywhere around me: the unexpected beauty of a breeze through the limbs of a tree, flowers in the cracks of sidewalks, or the friend who writes to tell me that He has given her a special word for me to hear.

You know, Jesus is always speaking. He is always near. His encouragement is bountiful and His strength within us is unfailing and unquenchable. I just need to have my *eyes* opened, expectant, and always on the lookout for what He is up to.

I do not want to miss anything He is saying and doing.

What Jesus is whispering to my heart today:

_____

_____

_____

_____

_____

July 17

Our sword in battle...

*And take the helmet of salvation and the sword of the Spirit, which is the*
*word of God;*
Ephesians 6:17

Yes, it is this God-breathed Word that brings healing to us, and this God-breathed Word that annihilates our adversary, the devil.

This sword, well, we gotta have a death grip on it. I mean, we have to have our hands, heads, and hearts so wrapped around it that no weapon of hell could ever pry it loose from us. *His Word* has *authority* - not our words – *His Word* on our lips that will wreak havoc on demon strongholds over people, situations, families, and nations.

Ask the Holy Spirit to give you a passage of Scripture for what burdens your heart. He will give it to you. Then speak it over what troubles you – praying and speaking in the name of Jesus. Keep declaring and praying as the Spirit leads you. Let God ignite this sword that you wield because it is your ammunition – your only ammunition.

It is time to grab this sword and not let go.

What Jesus is whispering to my heart today:

_____
_____
_____
_____
_____

# July 18

In the midst of this week...

If your stocks have dropped, your smile has drooped, you've locked your keys in the car, and your dog isn't sure if she likes you anymore, look up! There is ONE who knows the number of hairs on your head, Who knows you inside-out and loves you beyond reason. His love never fails!
1 Corinthians 13:8

Should you have a disagreement with a loved one, co-worker, classmate, housemate, in-law, or out-law, forgive quickly! Check your own heart first before you decide to check out of the situation. Make amends. Jesus has forgiven you everything. Let His grace in you spill onto someone else.
Matthew 18:22

This is a week of new beginnings, hopes to be realized, and miracles to watch for. Keep your eyes open, your heart tender, and your mind from distraction. This week will be awesome in Jesus because He Who is in you is greater than anything!
1 John 4:4

What Jesus is whispering to my heart today:

_____

_____

_____

_____

_____

July 19

The Lord Jesus is jealous for your love.

*For the LORD your God is a consuming fire, a jealous God.*
Deuteronomy 4:24

It is not that He won't bless the relationships you have, yet He won't compete with them either. It's not that He won't bless your hobbies or the way you relax, but He knows only true peace and fulfillment comes from His presence. He wants all your affection, all of your thoughts, and all of your heart.

When you struggled with past issues that you knew only He could resolve, you most likely tasted what it was like to hang onto Him for your every breath to get you through the day. He longs for you to be desperate for Him again in the good seasons of life as well. He is a jealous God. He loves you passionately, furiously, and intentionally. You won't find what you are looking for anywhere or in anyone else.

So just a reminder. You have been marked for His Kingdom to do great things, so nothing else is going to satisfy you. Others can get by with a tame Christianity, but you can't.

You are marked by His love. Don't settle for less.

What Jesus is whispering to my heart today:

_____

_____

_____

_____

_____

July 20

God's grace is like His manna from heaven; we will always have more than enough.

*And He said to me, "My grace is sufficient for you, for My strength is made perfect in weakness." Therefore most gladly I will rather boast in my infirmities, that the power of Christ may rest upon me.*
2 Corinthians 12:9

In *Exodus 16*, God told Israel that He would supply what they needed daily when they were hungry. Those that tried to horde the heavenly food found it went rancid overnight. Those who listened to Him and trusted He knew what He was doing and would take care of them completely had more than enough. They had an abundance of the heavenly gift.

The same is true with God's grace. We never have to fear His grace will run out either, just like the heavenly manna didn't run out. And because that is true, He won't let us horde it. Jesus wants us to come to Him daily to receive this all-plentiful feast. When the pressure is on in our lives, we will find that we will have double and triple portions from the bounty of grace from His lavish love.

Today, how about you and I gather some overwhelming grace. It will always be exactly what we need and more than we could ever hope for.

What Jesus is whispering to my heart today:

_____

_____

_____

_____

_____

July 25

In the midst of this week...

Should you need to forgive someone, no matter how slight or large the offense, get to it pronto!! Ask for Jesus' help. He has completely forgiven you and He *will* give you the strength to forgive others.
*Matthew 18:22*

Should you feel hemmed in by your circumstances, walls on every side, look up! Let God scoop you up in His everlasting arms and give you all that you need. He may have you surrounded for a strategic purpose, so don't try to wrangle out of what you are going through. Let Him carry you safely to your next destination in Him.
*Psalm 139:5*

This is a week of new beginnings, hopes to be realized, and miracles to watch for. Keep your eyes open, your heart tender, and your mind from distraction. This week will be awesome in Jesus because He Who is in you is greater than anything!
*1 John 4:4*

What Jesus is whispering to my heart today:

_____

_____

_____

_____

_____

July 26

I never knew I would like to write...

*You are worthy, O Lord, to receive glory and honor and power: for You*
*have created all things, and for Your pleasure they are and were created.*
Revelation 4:11

Writing was never on my life's radar even though I am an avid reader.
Nevertheless, in these last few years, I have discovered I love to write
about Jesus. I know enough to know that my prose is not all that great.
Still, Jesus loves my writing – I sense His pleasure when I tap out words
on my keyboard.

Every single one of us were created by Him and we bring Him such great
delight. And yes, you *are* His delight. So when we give the Holy Spirit
permission to take us out of our comfort zones and nurture us in
expressions of creativity and wonder that bring God exquisite delight, we
feel such pleasure, too.

Yes, we sense satisfaction, fulfillment, and purpose when we explore the
gifts and treasures He has given to each us, even though we may feel
insecure and fumbling at first. Remember, His talents within us are for an
audience of One and He will shout, *Bravo!* every time we try.

What Jesus is whispering to my heart today:

_____

_____

_____

_____

_____

# July 27

This little verse turned my world right side up...

*He who sins is of the devil, for the devil has sinned from the beginning. For this purpose the Son of God was manifested, that He might destroy the works of the devil.*
1 John 3:8

The Greek word used here for *destroy* is **lyo**: to loosen any person or thing that is tied or fastened, to loosen one that is bound; to set free.

I was someone who was tied up in knots for years. No, I wasn't the anxious type – I am a southern California beach girl through and through with the matching personality. Yet, I was twisted in the enemy's knots and lies about my worth: my appearance and my abilities.

If you are struggling today, get help, help, help. Don't delay! Most of all, seek the Good Shepherd who came to untie the knots of any and everything the devil, the world, others, and your own flesh may have bound and entangled you with.

He is more than able. He is more than willing. He loves you more than you will ever know, and He can untie every knot you find yourself caught in.

What Jesus is whispering to my heart today:

_____

_____

_____

_____

_____

# July 28

I came to know the Lord Jesus because of great *need* in my life…

*He who dwells in the secret place of the Most High shall remain stable
and fixed under the shadow of the Almighty (Whose power no foe can
withstand).*
Psalm 91:1 AMP

You know what? Coming to Him out of our need is okay. Our need is
fulfilled in His ability to turn our *mountains* into level plains, to heal our
sickness – physical, mental, emotional, and spiritual – and our need for
His love to fill our lives.

Nevertheless, at some point, the Holy Spirit nudges us to love the Lord
Jesus simply *for Who He is*, not what we can *get* from Him. This nudge
happened for me not so many years ago and I never want to go back.
Yes, life gets in the way and I get distracted. Yet, in His presence,
overwhelming stuff that comes my way just doesn't have the ability to
bowl me over like it once did.

Yes, all of Psalm 91 is awesome and its promises are for everyone, but
the condition is a daily, deeply abiding in-love relationship with the
Creator. What could be more wonder-filled?

What Jesus is whispering to my heart today:

_____

_____

_____

_____

_____

# July 29

What does Chef Julia Child have to do with the study of God's Word?

*Be diligent to present yourself approved to God, a worker who does not need to be ashamed, rightly dividing the word of truth.*
2 Timothy 2:15

Recently, while reading her autobiography, *My Life in France,* I became entranced with Julia's study, devotion and diligence to create the perfect mayonnaise. Mayonnaise! Her desperation to learn speaks to me.

In the verse above, the King James Version of the Bible uses the wording *study to show yourself approved.* The original Greek here tells us *to make haste or hasten*; speaking of an urgency to pour over, soak in, dissect, analyze, be steadfast in, and dive into God's Word.

Yes, devotional reading – reading 'til your heart is warmed by the Spirit – is imperative to learning to discern His voice daily. Yet when we study, research, and diligently pursue the Scriptures, we will find the *hidden* gemstones revealing more of who God is - His incredible attributes, His work among men, and His lavish love for us and the world we live in.

Let's fall in love with His Word and let it create in us an insatiable hunger for *more.*

What Jesus is whispering to my heart today:

_____

_____

_____

_____

_____

# July 30

I'm not looking over my shoulder anymore...

*But Jesus said to him, "No one, having put his hand to the plow, and looking back, is fit for the kingdom of God.*
Luke 9:62

This verse reminds me of Lot's wife who was commanded to not look back over her shoulder *Genesis 19:22*. Yet, she could not resist and because of looking back to her past, *she could not grasp her future.* She became a pillar of salt; forever *frozen* between what once was and the amazing prospects God was propelling her toward.

Looking back to our past, even if it has been painful, can sure be *comfortable*. Comfortable because it is familiar. We may not verbalize it, but sometimes what is familiar – even if it was hellish – is easier than trusting Jesus that He knows what is best for our *future*.

Even if our past is full of the miraculous of God's mighty hand, we can become frozen. However, the Spirit spurs us on. We only have to remember that Jesus kept the best wine for last. Life in Him only gets more exciting, fulfilling, and rewarding. So...

I don't want to look back to my past anymore. How about you?

What Jesus is whispering to my heart today:

_____

_____

_____

_____

_____

# July 31

Honestly. We can be in His Word daily, but still miss Him entirely...

*But be doers of the word, and not hearers only, deceiving yourselves.*
James 1:19

The Scriptures come alive in me when they are ignited, activated, and empowered by a fresh daily walk with Jesus up-close and personal. Not merely words on a page, the Bible contains the very breath of the Holy Spirit. We need to ask His help to overwhelm our souls with His presence, as well as ask His help to *do* what He speaks to us through His Word, such as:

*Don't worry.* Somehow, I think He means it.
*Abide, remain, drink deeply in Me.* This is an invitation to share in His peace, joy, happiness, and love beyond compare.
*Take up your cross daily.* Not just when it is convenient.
*I am worthy of your trust.* At all times. Period.

Let's read and apply His Word, be wrecked by His Holy Spirit, and walk in tight, daily communion with the God of the Universe. Now this is living!

What Jesus is whispering to my heart today:

_____

_____

_____

_____

_____

# August 1

In the midst of this week...

If your goldfish has kicked the bucket, your car is on its last leg, and your best friend won't return your texts, it is time to get alone with the Great Comforter. Ask the Holy Spirit what is really going on and be quiet and still to hear His voice. He will guide you into your next steps for all these situations. He will!
*John 14:16*

If your health, finances, or future are in question, it is time to turn to God's Word. What does He say about your situation? He will make a way through the wilderness, but it needs to be *His* way, not yours.
*Isaiah 43:20*

This is a week of new beginnings, hopes to be realized, and miracles to watch for. Keep your eyes open, your heart tender, and your mind from distraction. This week will be awesome in Jesus because He Who is in you is greater than anything!
*1 John 4:4*

What Jesus is whispering to my heart today:

_____

_____

_____

_____

_____

# August 2

My secret is simple. I pray...

*...praying always with all prayer and supplication in the Spirit, being watchful to this end with all perseverance and supplication for all the saint.* Ephesians 6:18

Prayer comes as the final piece of spiritual armor that Paul describes in *Ephesians 6:10-20.* We can't live life without it.

A quote from the president of Every Home for Christ, Dick Eastman, is the finest summation of prayer and spiritual warfare I have ever read regarding Paul's words to the church...

*To put on the armor of God is to prepare for battle. However, prayer is not so much a weapon, or even a part of the armor, as it is the means by which we engage in the battle itself and the purpose for which we are armed. Prayer is the battle itself, with God's Word being our chief weapon employed against Satan during our struggle.*

Enough said

What Jesus is whispering to my heart today:

_____

_____

_____

_____

_____

# August 3

We have been invited to a party...

*He brought me to the banqueting house,*
*And His banner over me was love.*
Song of Solomon 2:3-4

Have you been attending *less-than* kinds of festivities? Well, our God is
presenting us with a feast – an off-the-charts banquet – every day of our
lives. It is when we *do not* accept His invitation that we miss out. Simply
read *Luke 15:31* to sear that truth to your soul.

He calls us to the satisfying and joy-filled wonder of the feast of His
Word and the presence of the Holy Spirit. No matter what we face
in *this* moment – challenging or fun-filled; tragic or deliriously happy –
His feast awaits, free of charge *Isaiah 55:1-2*.

It is the only party where we can find fulfillment, satisfaction, true
happiness, and beyond-reason love. His table is *always* set, and a place
with our name on it is always reserved. When we accept His invitation,
we enter His courts with the banner of His love flying high over our
heads. Come, let's join the Master. He is awaiting us with open arms.


What Jesus is whispering to my heart today:

_____

_____

_____

_____

_____

# August 4

Fall hard *into* grace…

*You have become estranged from Christ, you who attempt to be justified by law; you have fallen from grace.*
Galatians 5:4

Have you, like me, been impatient, tempted, or tried and failed at something today? Are you worried or anxious, though you clearly know Jesus can be trusted to walk with you through whatever you face?

These things, well, sometimes they can make us wonder if we are walking closely at all with the Lord Jesus. And yet, He calls to us to *fall hard into His grace.*

No matter what has taken place today, His grace is sufficient to cover our lack, our weakness, and yes, our sin. Paul is telling us we *fall* from grace *only* when we *forget* His grace. A fall from this free gift is *not* blowing it so badly that we have exhausted it. That is impossible. No, a fall from His grace only happens when we *try to earn* this amazing, boundless gift.

What freedom. What joy. What power to actually live transformed lives. Yes, let's fall hard *into* His amazing grace.

What Jesus is whispering to my heart today:

_____

_____

_____

_____

_____

# August 5

I am generally willing or obedient, but not usually both together!

*If you are willing and obedient,*
*You shall eat the good of the land;*
Isaiah 1:19

From *James 3:17* we learn the phrase *willing to yield* is a huge part of the believer's life. We are to be *willing* to yield our lives to Jesus and His plans, His work, His desires without a moment's hesitation on our part.

Often, *obedience* sounds like such a harsh word – until a person becomes a parent and then it becomes music to their ears! The definition of *obedience* is *to watchfully and carefully listen and follow through with matching behavior to instructions given by someone.*

What is the promise for when we are willing and obedient? We will eat the *goodness, prosperity, joy,* and *peace* of the land; the land of our lives

Ah, yes. Willing to yield and quick to obey. Please help me, Holy Spirit

What Jesus is whispering to my heart today:

_____

_____

_____

_____

_____

# August 6

True confessions...

*...Do not sorrow, for the joy of the LORD is your strength.*
Nehemiah 8:10b

I have spent the last few weeks in a quandary of my own flesh and the devil's making. I let the joy of the Lord be stolen from me in my daily workplace.

I had been struggling with trying to juggle a forty-hour work week in a secular marketplace with other avenues of ministry the Lord had called me to. I was starting to think God needed me more in those ministry scenarios. I lost my joy for what I was truly created for: a marketplace ministry and praying with people one-on-one, especially non-believers.

Are you being robbed of joy today? If so, give it to Jesus. Let *Him* call the plays. Break the agreements you have been making with the enemy because of your grumbling and complaining. Change your tune and ask the Holy Spirit to flood you with fresh joy – Jesus' joy. I am doing this right now.

What Jesus is whispering to my heart today:

_____

_____

_____

_____

_____

# August 7

Jesus always levels the playing field…

*And He came down with them and stood on a level place with a crowd of His disciples and a great multitude of people…who came to hear Him and be healed of their diseases.*
 Luke 6:17

The fact that the King of the Universe stoops to our level to be near us is beyond comprehension.

We live in a day of platform, position, and plaudits. The higher the celebrity profile, the better. Yet, Jesus always comes down to our level and meets us right where we are in the midst of our stuff, our selfishness, and yes, our sin.

And I love that, with the King of the Universe, the playing field of life is level. We come as we are because He is all-sufficient, and we are not. In His eyes, no one is better, higher, smarter, or more loved by Him. We don't ever have to fear not being enough or that someone else is more…

We simply come and are healed.

What Jesus is whispering to my heart today:

_____

_____

_____

_____

_____

# August 8

In the midst of this week...

If your hope is drooping, your faith is dropping, and your joy has already flown out the window; this is the perfect time to dig into Jesus' words about abiding in Him. Basically, you can't do life without *Him*! It's time to get back on track and fully lean, rely, and put your whole trust in the LORD.
*John 15:1-17*

On the other hand, if it is your bank account that is drooping, your stock options are dropping, or your next paycheck has already flown out the window; it may be time to take inventory. You may have to make some hard decisions about spending. Yet, King Jesus is oh so trustworthy. He takes care of the flowers and birds and He will take care of you!
*Matthew 6:25-34*

This is a week of new beginnings, hopes to be realized, and miracles to watch for. Keep your eyes open, your heart tender, and your mind from distraction. This week will be awesome in Jesus because He Who is in you is greater than anything!
*1 John 4:4*

What Jesus is whispering to my heart today:

_____

_____

_____

_____

# August 9

I just experienced something wonder-filled...

*For God so loved the world that He gave His only begotten Son, that whoever believes in Him should not perish but have everlasting life.* John 3:16

Just now, I came from a meeting with a brand new believer in Jesus. We have been meeting in that great discipleship gathering place: MickyD's. This beautiful, mature woman just read *John 3:16* for the very first time in her life.

This verse which contains the whole of the gospel will never lose its *punch* or its tenderness. The heart of God was poured out for His wayward children – for God so loved.

Two things: *Who* do you have in your life that needs someone to either walk with them in their Journey *to* Jesus or *in* Jesus?

Second: Those precious, most powerful words say it all, don't they?

What Jesus is whispering to my heart today:

_____

_____

_____

_____

_____

# August 10

Anybody feeling just a little overwhelmed right now?

*From the end of the earth I will cry to You,*
*When my heart is overwhelmed;*
*Lead me to the rock that is higher than I.*
Psalm 61:2

Too much stuff to do, too little time to do it? So many dreams, but not enough money to accomplish them? Join the club. I think most of mankind is feeling a little overwhelmed.

Nevertheless, King David tells us *what* to do and *Who* to go to. That simple. *Cry out!* he tells us. *Cry out* to your heavenly Father who loves you beyond reason. Go to your room and pour out your heart; lay it all out before Him. Then wait.

Wait for the Holy Spirit to lift your gaze, your heart, and your spirit to THE ROCK – the Rock of Ages. Jesus hasn't moved, been shaken, or ever wavered. As He bends down to take you by the hand, look up as He draws you to Himself in safety. You will find rest, peace, and direction for your soul and for your life.

What Jesus is whispering to my heart today:

_____

_____

_____

_____

# August 11

Oh my, the daily news from around the world is daunting...

*Peace I leave with you, My peace I give to you; not as the world gives do I give to you. Let not your heart be troubled, neither let it be afraid.*
John 14:27

It is the church's propensity to come under *fear* that concerns me. Especially when His Word tells us the days will grow darker before the dawn of Jesus' return.

From countless Scriptures we learn that fear and anxiety are *not* our portion. Fear is *not* who we are in Him. If fear arises in us, we then have to ask the Holy Spirit what it is we really are afraid of. What is the *lie* we are believing because Jesus *is* LORD.

As the world grows darker, Jesus in us shines brighter. This is our hour to intercede and battle in prayer for regions around the globe in tremendous turmoil. This is our hour to pray heaven down, just as He taught us *Matthew 6:10*. When we don't know how to pray, let's pray in the Holy Spirit's language He has given us.

So, let's pray hard, love *everyone* tenaciously, expect the miraculous, and lead souls to Christ, the Prince of Peace.

What Jesus is whispering to my heart today:

_____

_____

_____

_____

_____

# August 12

How about making the passage below become your verse for this week?

*They looked to Him and were radiant,*
*And their faces were not ashamed.*
Psalm 34:5

Almost all of us have some degree of shame in our lives. Even the seemingly most proud person is usually over-compensating for because of sense of shame somewhere in their soul.

In Christ alone, the spirit of shame can be broken. Certainly, the affirmation and encouragement of others goes a long way to bring restoration. And yes, some self-bolstering and our accomplishments, small or large, help us greatly, but only the Lord Jesus can truly, genuinely, and thoroughly *heal* shame.

So, if this is your struggle today, or on occasion, seek the Lord's face. Let His words sink in and heal your heart and mind; freeing you from the torment of shame and its lies. This may be a process of deliverance from this tyrant, but let the radiance of His life begin in you today.

What Jesus is whispering to my heart today:

_____
_____
_____
_____
_____

# August 13

Oh my, I received two magazines in my mail today...

*My soul, wait silently for God alone,*
*For my expectation is from Him.*
Psalms 62:5

The first magazine stated confidently on the cover: *The Best New Products to Make Your life Better.* The second magazine declared: *Six Trips that will Change Your Life!*

If only. Why is it that I – and the magazine industry – look to externals to mend and fix what only the Holy Spirit can tenderly heal? Will a product really make my life better? Can a trip change my life for the long haul and not just for the week when I don't have to do laundry?

Through trial and error, I have found that life only dramatically changes for the unimaginably better when I live in the truth of the verse above. Because then I stop putting false and exhausting expectations on *myself* that I can rarely rise to. It is then that I release loved ones from my selfish expectations and set them free to be loved unconditionally by me. Then finally, I realize that outside circumstances cannot bring fulfillment and significance to the deep vacuum of my heart.

Yes, Jesus alone has exceeded all of my heart's expectations.

What Jesus is whispering to my heart today:

_____

_____

_____

_____

_____

# August 14

These words recently leapt off the pages of my Bible and landed directly into my heart...

*Watch, stand fast in the faith,*
*be brave, be strong.*
*Let all that you do be done with love.*
1 Corinthians 16:13-14

The Holy Spirit is whispering for me to watch and guard my heart from the world's ensnarement. I am also to watch for what He is doing and partner with Him to bring Jesus to those in need of Him.

He is calling me to ruthlessly believe His Word. To believe Him with no more *Plan B's*. And because I want the Holy Spirit to super-naturally enable me for what He has put before me, I need His bravery and His strength, not mine. Lastly, I yearn for everything I do to be done in His *agape* love. This is a tall order that only He can fulfill. I believe He will.

Do you need some verses to be your personal mission statement for the next few days, few months, or maybe the rest of your life? These words would be a great place to start.

What Jesus is whispering to my heart today:

_____

_____

_____

_____

_____

# August 15

In the midst of this week...

Should you feel discouraged about something, and you just can't seem to shake it off your heart, it is time to seek the face of the Heart Healer. Really. Go to a private place and pour your heart out to Him. Take a look at *Psalm 102*. Don't leave His presence until you sense the Holy Spirit lifting your burden.

Should you be weary of a continuing behavior that you just can't seem to gain freedom from, don't give up. Let *Psalm 18* minister to you. Talk to your pastor or seek a gifted prayer warrior to go to battle for you. Jesus wants you *well*, *whole,* and *free.*

This is a week of new beginnings, hopes to be realized, and miracles to watch for. Keep your eyes open, your heart tender, and your mind from distraction. This week will be awesome in Jesus because He Who is in you is greater than anything!
*1 John 4:4*

What Jesus is whispering to my heart today:

_____

_____

_____

_____

_____

# August 16

You never know how Jesus might work...

*"For My thoughts are not your thoughts,*
*Nor are your ways My ways," says the LORD.*
 Isaiah 55:8

I am visiting my elderly dad today. I took a walk past the church building where Jesus came to rescue me as young girl; where He baptized me in the Holy Spirit when I was a teenager and where I sensed His call to ministry that redirected the trajectory of my life.

I am so thankful He works in ways we can't figure out. It was the seemingly random choice that my parents made to buy a humble home, in a then humble neighborhood, that had such an impact on a young life. This amazes me.

He has the details of your life in His hands, too. If some things are still a puzzle, don't worry. Jesus knows what He is doing and He always knows best. So, trust Him with every detail, listen for His whisper of direction and act upon it. Then, stand back and watch Him create a masterpiece.

What Jesus is whispering to my heart today:

_____

_____

_____

_____

_____

# August 17

Jesus called it...

*These things I have spoken to you, that in Me you may have peace. In the world you will have tribulation; but be of good cheer, I have overcome the world.*
John 16:33

We live in a messed up world and the King of Kings has no problem naming the devil as the culprit of earth's darkness. However, this one who rules this planet *1 John 5:19*, the one who would kill, rob, and destroy, is no match for the One who came to give *life abundantly*. He is our Peace. He is...the Light of the World.

We need to start – if we haven't already – to take our stand on our knees. Let's be praying for those who don't know Jesus yet. Let's be praying for nations. And, let's be praying for the power of God's Word and the miraculous in the Holy Spirit to be multiplied so that many might come to faith. And, if we haven't done it yet, let's get serious about our own walk with the Lord.

One thing is for sure. In the midst of overwhelming darkness His Light shines brighter still.

What Jesus is whispering to my heart today:

_____

_____

_____

_____

_____

# August 18

All of us have experienced rejection at some point in our lives…

*Even if my father and mother abandon me,*
*the LORD will hold me close.*
Psalm 27:10

There is nothing quite like the pain of feeling rejected. It may have occurred on a playground, or it may have been in a marriage. It may have stemmed from a parent's brokenness or not getting a much-anticipated dream job. From the slightest incident to the most horrendous – rejection is painful.

Jesus knows a lot about rejection. One only needs a cursory glance at the four Gospels to know this is true. However, there is no rejection and no abandonment in the pure-love-unity He has with the Father and the Holy Spirit. In *John 15,* He invites us into this love relationship with the Trinity. Oh my, what an incomprehensible invitation that we often *reject.*

It is time to get our eyes off our hurt that has often become our identity. It is time to solely look to Jesus for comfort and draw near to Him to heal these wounds. It is time to let Him hold us close and close the chapter on our pain. And yes, He can do this, and yes, it is time.

What Jesus is whispering to my heart today:

_____

_____

_____

_____

_____

# August 19

Here is a simple recipe for a Holy Spirit transformation in our lives...

*Don't copy the behavior and customs of this world, but let God transform you into a new person by changing the way you think. Then you will learn to know God's will for you, which is good and pleasing and perfect.* Romans 12:2 NLT

We need a complete paradigm shift, from the world's way of thinking, to Jesus' way of thinking. All that we encounter passes through our minds, even before reaching our emotions. Our thoughts affect everything regarding our perceptions of the people around us, our circumstances, ourselves, even our perceptions about God.

I was very much like the Charlie Brown character, Pig-Pen, and this is not a glamorous comparison! Nevertheless, the swirling mass of thoughts and confusion consuming most of my life was very much like the swirling mass of debris little Pig-Pen's life depicted. Jesus changed all that and He is still continually renewing my mind.

From this launching pad of freedom in my thoughts, I started realizing who I was created to be. My goodness, that's what Paul writes about next in *Romans 12*. Take a look and then get serious with the Holy Spirit about what you think regarding – everything.

What Jesus is whispering to my heart today:

_____

_____

_____

_____

_____

# August 24

We hear about *working* at our relationships. Nevertheless, when our faith life becomes *work*, we have to wonder...did we miss *Him* somewhere?

*Nevertheless I have this against you, that you have left your first love.*
Revelation 2:4

Instead of *working* at our relationship with Jesus, maybe we should think of *cultivating* or *nurturing* our communion with Him. Possibly, this is why the parable of the *Sower and the Seed* is repeated three times in His written Word.

Consider a tender seedling: you guard it, you care for it, and you protect it from exposure. You shelter it, water it, and feed it daily, if not hourly, because it is fragile. Our relationship with the Lord is fragile. It needs tending. No, it isn't fragile on *His* side of the equation, but it certainly is delicate on *our* side. And, it is opposed. Oh! So opposed! How the enemy loves to distract, sideline, and yes, destroy our first love for Him.

Where is your heart as you read this? Is your first love with Jesus a memory of your past? If so, simply remember His *first love* for you has never wavered. Simply return to Him, then guard what He ignites within you with all of your heart.

What Jesus is whispering to my heart today:

---

---

---

---

---

# August 25

I have a *Type A* personality, yet, because I am clothed in goofiness, I fool a lot of people. But not the Lord…

*So why do you worry about clothing? Consider the lilies of the field, how they grow: they neither toil nor spin;"*
Matthew 6:28

Last summer, my driven nature nearly sidetracked all Jesus was trying to do in my life. In July a friend had a *word* for me: the Lord desired for me to stop my hot pursuit of various ministries and rest in Him. Ouch! Two days later, at a small prayer gathering, the leader felt the Spirit's nudging to look up the original meanings of all our names. Ironically, my first name, Susan, literally means *Lily*. I wanted to be *Warrior*, *Princess*, or *Harvester*, which were some of the others' names meanings that evening.

The next morning, I turned to the verse above. I saw my name clearly in Jesus' words. *Toiling* and *spinning* are perfect definitions of a driven personality. I had to laugh. God *so* has my number.

Are you driven by, or about, something? Take it from *Lily*, here. Rest and let Him do the heavy lifting in your life. He is able to carry your load and mine, too.

What Jesus is whispering to my heart today:

_____

_____

_____

_____

_____

# August 26

There is a world of difference between simply reading the Bible and experiencing its power...

*Then Jesus said to those Jews who believed Him,*
*"If you abide in My word, you are My disciples indeed.*
*And you shall know the truth, and the truth shall make you free."*
John 8:31-32

My dear friend, Marjorie, shared with me yesterday...

Although she dearly and deeply loved God's Word for years, she once was riddled and held captive by every fear imaginable. Guilt and shame were weaved into her daily life, as well. It wasn't until she asked the Holy Spirit to breathe His inspired Word into her heart while she read, did she experience the *transforming work* of the Word. She began to encounter the power of Jesus, Living Word. Lies that she had once believed – that had caused so much fearful torment – began to be broken by God's truth. So...

Read the Bible to learn, learn, learn, but also ask the Spirit to cause life, deliverance, healing, and restoration be your daily experience, too.

What Jesus is whispering to my heart today:

_____

_____

_____

_____

_____

# August 27

*I want to do what I want to do...*

This is one of the scariest phrases I could ever hear someone utter. Why so scary? Because I have said or thought them and the consequences of this phrase almost cost me everything. I shudder when I hear these words spoken now or sense someone is taking a turn towards them in their life.

*And you must always obey the LORD's commands and decrees that I am giving you today for your own good.*
Deuteronomy 10:13 NLT (emphasis, mine)

God's Word, His commandments, and His guidance are not about thwarting our lives, derailing our dreams, or telling us not to have *fun*. His commands and decrees are all about how to live successfully, abundantly, and navigate prosperously in every way possible through this dark, evil, and weary world that the enemy controls. Don't be duped by the devil's lies thinking you know better than the Savior's life-giving Word. Your outcome could be devastating.

So when this thought comes your way, *I want to do what I want to do*, run for cover in the Savior's arms. Let Him show you His way. What He has in store for your life will be so much more extraordinary and better. And as the verse above states: *it will be good.*

What Jesus is whispering to my heart today:

_____

_____

_____

_____

_____

# August 28

I can only imagine what it must have felt like to have the Savior of the world call for you to come…

*So Jesus stood still and commanded him to be called. Then they called the blind man, saying to him, "Be of good cheer. Rise, He is calling you."* Mark 10:49

I was so moved by this passage as I read it today. Immediately I sensed the Holy Spirit gently reminding me that Lord Jesus is always calling me to come to Him.

I am one blessed woman. I can honestly say the Lord has granted me above what I have ever expected or dreamed of. His reality is ever so much better than any fantasy or imagination my mind could have come up with. So, this latter portion of my life I simply desire to be in His presence every moment of every day. When He calls my name, I want to come without hesitation. You, too?

Let's come away and sit alone with Jesus and His Word. Let's pray in the Spirit and be filled with His peace, presence, and power. Then, let's live in the Holy Spirit so that those around us hunger to come when He calls them, too.

If He is calling me. I know He is calling you. Simply answer His call.

What Jesus is whispering to my heart today:

_____

_____

_____

_____

_____

# August 29

In the midst of this week...

Should your car not start, your list of things-to-do won't stop, or a child, spouse, boss, or even the hamster is going sideways on you, it is time to truly hand your cares over to Jesus. And now get this – you will need to leave those cares there in His almighty, capable care. No taking them back!
*1 Peter 5:7*

Should you feel like complaining about all of the difficulties of your life, choose instead to celebrate that you have life at all! No matter what you are facing, the King of Glory has gone before you. Now, take His hand, speak praise, and dive into His Word. He is more than enough for whatever you need.
*James 5:13*

This is a week of new beginnings, hopes to be realized, and miracles to watch for. Keep your eyes open, your heart tender, and your mind from distraction. This week will be awesome in Jesus because He Who is in you is greater than anything!
*1 John 4:4*

What Jesus is whispering to my heart today:

_____

_____

_____

_____

_____

# August 30

Here is an interesting Scripture...

*To proclaim the acceptable year of the LORD, And the day of vengeance of our God; To comfort all who mourn.*
Isaiah 61:2

This verse almost sticks out like a sore thumb in the middle of one of the most beautiful and powerful passages in the Bible. But no. While foretelling the miraculous freedom and forgiveness to be found in the gospel of Jesus, God's day of vengeance is the lynchpin.

No, not vengeance against us, but toward our adversary, the devil. That liar's day of doom took place during the anguish of the cross. When Jesus cried out, *It is finished*, it not only meant our death sentence had been paid in full by His blood, but Jesus also secured our enemy's judgment. Yes, his final demise won't take place until Jesus comes again, but in the meantime...

We need to know who we are in Christ. We need to realize the authority He has given us. We need to remember that our enemy bows to Jesus' name. We need to start walking in all we learn from God's Word about who we are in Christ.

What Jesus is whispering to my heart today:

_____

_____

_____

_____

_____

# August 31

Oh my. A little gratefulness and a little praise time can do so much...

*But at midnight Paul and Silas were praying and singing hymns to God,
and the prisoners were listening to them.*
Acts 16:25

The Book of Acts is about real people, with real stuff, real trials, and an
ever-present God Who works real miracles. Nothing has changed.

I am a real person, with real stuff, and real trials, but God remains bigger
still. You know, a little cup of thankfulness can break the enemy's back
in our lives. A sentence of genuine worship can move mountains. A
grateful heart declaring God is good, loves us to pieces, and is ever for
us, speaks a death knell for chains of bondage.

What do you face today? Instead of dwelling upon it, remember Paul and
Silas. Pray. Praise. Look to the One who loves you so very much.

See heaven move in your heart and your circumstances.

What Jesus is whispering to my heart today:

_____

_____

_____

_____

_____

# September 1

Life begins at the end of your comfort zone...

*But without faith it is impossible to please Him,*
*for he who comes to God must believe that He is,*
*and that He is a rewarder of those who diligently seek Him.*
Hebrews 11:6

Anna Finfrock, a young American friend of mine whom I met in Taiwan, posted this opening sentence on Instagram today. She and her husband are now serving the Lord in South Africa and yep, it's true...

*Faith in Jesus* is rubber-meets-the-road time when it comes to bringing Him great pleasure. Faith involves trust, and trust is the highest form of adoration. Nevertheless, faith *always* requires risk.

This is not risk or leaving our comfort zone for the sake of being stupid or trying to prove something. But when He calls my name and His invitation invites risk, it is not time to shrink back, hold back, or think of my comfort. I have had plenty of comfort in my life – *booooring*! But His thrill-ride these past twelve years has been amazing, exciting, miraculous, and wonder-filled. Could Jesus do anything less?

Nope. So, I am willing to leave my comfort zone when He calls. Will you join me?

What Jesus is whispering to my heart today:

_____

_____

_____

_____

_____

# September 2

We live in a numbers obsessed world...

*Then the LORD said to Gideon, "By the three hundred men who lapped I will save you, and deliver the Midianites into your hand..."*
Judges 7:7a

Except for the bathroom scale, the higher the number – the better: followers, likes, church attendance. However, God isn't hung-up with numbers like we can be. Ahem...like I can be.

The Lord whittled Gideon's army from 32,000 to 300 men. God alone was going to rout the Midianites. He doesn't need numbers to accomplish His plans. From the Scriptures we learn that He is simply looking for open, tender, faith-filled hearts. And then, watch out for His miraculous workings that do not need human strength.

Yes, numbers are a good way to inventory what is happening, but not the only way. And, one hungry life following after the One and Only is all Jesus needs.

Sign me up, Lord!

What Jesus is whispering to my heart today:

_____

_____

_____

_____

_____

# September 3

When I heard about my two friends reconciling after hitting a rough patch in their relationship, it brought me to tears and I remembered this portion of the Lord's Prayer...

*And forgive us our debts,*
*As we forgive our debtors.*
Matthew 6:12

Really. Honestly. When I truly see my own brokenness, failings, and failures, I can more readily forgive others. I wouldn't have thought this true. Yet as the Lord began to heal me from the inside-out of my own shame, insecurities, wounds, hurts, and addictions – I couldn't hold blame over anyone else's life.

I also made the wondrous discovery that spending a little bit of time in Jesus' overwhelming presence filled my soul to overflowing. From these shared moments with the Savior, I realized that *stuff* which would have previously wounded my heart, just didn't have that power any longer.

*Hurt people – hurt people.* Nevertheless, when Jesus forgives, heals, and transforms us, we learn that *forgiven people can forgive people.* I want to live this way. You too?


What Jesus is whispering to my heart today:

_____

_____

_____

_____

_____

# September 4

One of the most significant aspects of the Gospel is His healing for the brokenness we experience in the deep recesses of our lives…

*Search me, O God, and know my heart;*
*Try me, and know my anxieties;*
*And see if there is any wicked way in me,*
*And lead me in the way everlasting.*
Psalm 139:23-24

We need never fear the Holy Spirit's searchlight into our innermost being – our hearts and minds. He can wade through all the muck and mire; shame and pride; lust and selfishness. Jesus longs to bring us into His freedom and wholeness. He never once stops loving us, no matter what His searchlight reveals. He is with us in those dark places.

If we are tired of living with anxiety, insecurity, bondage to habits we disdain, and a myriad of other soul-sicknesses, the verse above is the launching point to release in our lives. Let's let Jesus go deep in our souls and allow His truth to reveal the lies we believe about ourselves. Let's take some time before this day ends to meet with the Great Counselor to start this incredible journey of freedom. He is able, and He is waiting for us to come and experience His healing, tender touch.

What Jesus is whispering to my heart today:

_____

_____

_____

_____

_____

# September 5

In the midst of this week...

Should it feel like the walls are closing in, your pathway is blocked, or you are stumped about what to do in a particular situation, it is time to speak God's truth over your life. He is the one who is above, below, behind, and in front of you – not your enemy, the devil. Rebuke that liar in Jesus' Name and declare *Psalm 139* out loud over your life.

Should your heart be gloomy, downcast, or just plain in the dumps, remember Whose child you are. You are the King's kid! Run to His throne – not your phone – to find all you need to face any situation. Jesus rules!
*Hebrews 4:16*

This is a week of new beginnings, hopes to be realized, and miracles to watch for. Keep your eyes open, your heart tender, and your mind from distraction. This week will be awesome in Jesus because He Who is in you is greater than anything!
*1 John 4:4*

What Jesus is whispering to my heart today:

_____

_____

_____

_____

_____

# September 6

Jesus' resurrection was not the culmination of the Greatest Story ever told, it was the beginning...

*The former account I made, O Theophilus,*
*of all that Jesus began both to do and teach,*
Acts 1:1

The Book of Acts from God's Word chronicles just a few of the many wondrous accounts of Christ's Body – the church – filled with the power of the Holy Spirit. It is now *our* story.

Should your life seem somehow dull, unsatisfying, not quite fulfilling, or thrilling, take a look again at this book in the Bible. There you will find rubber-meets-the-road accounts of faith in action. You will discover broken, sin-scarred, messed up people who were transformed, healed, and set free by His love and then unleashed upon the world. In my darkest hours of soul-sickness, the truth of these accounts caused me to know there was more for my life.

Jesus is doing it. I am a novice in faith – though I have been a Christian a long time – but I have seen too many miracles to turn back now. Each day is a new beginning in the overflow and baptism of the Holy Spirit and *yes Lord*, is all I need to say.

What Jesus is whispering to my heart today:

_____

_____

_____

_____

_____

# September 7

Have you ever followed the Lord's leading then hit a storm of adversity?

*Now it happened, on a certain day,*
*that He got into a boat with His disciples.*
*And He said to them, "Let us cross over to the other side of the lake."*
*And they launched out.*
Luke 8:22

Here Jesus tells the disciples to head to the other side of the Sea of Galilee and He promptly goes to sleep. As they cross this body of water – as He instructed – a severe windstorm whips up, and their boat takes on water. They are perishing.

Yet, *HIS* word never changed. They *did* make it to the other side. The disciples thought He didn't care – yet He never left them. They were shaken, fearful, and despairing – Jesus was not. I am sure they would have preferred calm waters, but what a story!

If you are going through something similar, take a look at Luke 8. You will be encouraged, and you will reach His destination for you.

Continue to launch out.


What Jesus is whispering to my heart today:

_____

_____

_____

_____

_____

# September 8

I am *wrecked* for Jesus...

*So I said: "Woe is me, for I am undone! Because I am a man of unclean lips, And I dwell in the midst of a people of unclean lips; For my eyes have seen the King, The LORD of hosts."*
Isaiah 6:5

I was doing my usual work stuff today – payroll for a hundred-plus folks, setting up a luncheon, scheduling my chief's calendar, and any and everything for a busy medical center – when the verse above came to mind. I sensed the Holy Spirit profoundly within and I again came to the realization that I am wrecked for Jesus. Just as the old prophet states: I am undone.

Really. Who or what else is there to live for? I spent the first decades of my life with Jesus on the sidelines. Never mind that I was involved in full-time pastoral ministry. You can do that, you know: serve Jesus, but still not lose your life for Him. That was me; but no more.

Life begins when I am *wrecked* for Him – living for what He says, what He does, not listening to this fallen world, and not hesitating when He calls.

What Jesus is whispering to my heart today:

_____

_____

_____

_____

_____

# September 9

Often, Jesus is calling us to go deeper than we want to go…

*When He had stopped speaking, He said to Simon,*
*"Launch out into the deep*
*and let down your nets for a catch."*
Luke 5:4

Recently, my son-in-law stated: *I wish everything didn't always require faith!* We laughed out loud. How many times have we felt the same way?

Nevertheless, when we signed up with Jesus – you know – invited Him to be Lord of our lives – we stepped from the realm of controlling our destiny to fully trusting Him. And that requires our *faith*. Often, He calls us into the deep waters of trust rather than safely standing on the shore, missing the adventure – missing Him.

What area of your life is Jesus calling you to a deeper trust in regarding its outcome? Don't delay in responding to Him. Just read the rest of *Luke 5* and see the splendor of what He can do in your situation.

What Jesus is whispering to my heart today:

_____

_____

_____

_____

_____

# September 10

An old, familiar verse came to mind this morning…

*You will keep him in perfect peace,*
*Whose mind is stayed on You,*
*Because he trusts in You.*
Isaiah 26:3

I am remembering that the same Hebrew word, *shalom,* is used *twice* here in the original text for *perfect* and *peace*. The Lord is making a point.

*Shalom, shalom*! Perfect peace! Peace, peace! A double-portion of His peace.

*Shalom* (Hebrew), meaning completeness, wholeness, peace, health, welfare, safety, soundness, tranquility, prosperity, perfectness, fullness, rest, and harmony.

Do you need one *shalom* in your life right now, or two? Choose to trust Him completely and strengthen your faith by setting your mind upon who He is and the promises of His Word. A double-scoop of His incomprehensible *shalom* will be yours.

What Jesus is whispering to my heart today:

_____

_____

_____

_____

_____

# September 11

What one thing has the ability to poison our soul? *Comparison…*

*Jesus said to him, "If I will that he remain till I come, what is that to you? You follow Me."*
John 21:22

Yes, of course one could add the poison of jealousy, bitterness, envy, or hatred in our hearts, but *comparison* is oh so seductive. No matter what our age, ethnicity, or gender, when we begin the slippery slope of comparing any aspect of our lives with someone else, our joy is diminished, our insecurities reign, and jealousy, bitterness, and every kind of no-good emotion can take ground in our hearts.

Peter was taking his gaze off the Savior and placing it onto someone else. We tend to do the same thing too. Yet, when we look to the right or the left of us, we will always come up short. Take it from one who was an expert at doing this. However, it will never happen if we set the gaze of our hearts on Jesus alone. Only He can satisfy our souls, bring significance to our lives, and meet every longing of our hungry hearts.

*You follow Me.* I am coming, Lord, following You alone!


What Jesus is whispering to my heart today:

_____

_____

_____

_____

_____

# September 12

In the midst of this week....

Should your favorite sports team lose, or your team didn't even come close to even making a good showing, remember that you are on the winning team in Jesus. That is all that matters. If your head knows this truth, but your heart hasn't caught up, it is time to put faith in action. Get back into His Word. Be encouraged to *believe* Him.
*Revelation 12:11*

Should your hope be sagging, your strength is waning, or your joy has disappeared somewhere, it is time to get alone and be quiet with the only One who can satisfy your every need. His presence is the air you breathe, and His Word is the rock that holds you up. Quit your busyness and get still with Him. Anything less is pointless and a waste of time. Really. Truly.
*Isaiah 40:31*

This is a week of new beginnings, hopes to be realized, and miracles to watch for. Keep your eyes open, your heart tender, and your mind from distraction. This week will be awesome in Jesus because He Who is in you is greater than anything!
*1 John 4:4*

What Jesus is whispering to my heart today:

_____

_____

_____

_____

_____

# September 13

A little light goes a long way…

*If we say that we have fellowship with Him, and walk in darkness, we lie and do not practice the truth.*
1 John 1:6

There is a lot to be said about bringing our stuff into the light. You know, the stuff we would really rather keep hidden – the stuff we are ashamed of, but we don't know how to free ourselves from. The enemy's tactics usually win here in our lives: isolation, keeping our issues to ourselves, entertaining a fear of rejection or of being judged regarding our stuff. However, the next verse encourages us to step *forward*.

*But if we walk in the light as He is in the light, we have fellowship with one another, and the blood of Jesus Christ His Son cleanses us from all sin.*
1 John 1:6-7

Jesus cleansing us also means His freedom. Truly free. If you are hiding something, it is time to bring it into His glorious, loving, blazing, piercing, but tender *light*.

What Jesus is whispering to my heart today:

_____

_____

_____

_____

_____

# September 14

People really are messed up, no matter where they live...

*I will also tear off your veils and deliver My people out of your hand...*
*Because with lies you have made the heart of the righteous sad, whom I*
*have not made sad...*
Ezekiel 13:21-22

I live in a pretty rough city. In the state of California, my town is not on
the Top Ten best places to live. You don't see tour buses stopping here to
see the sights. You get my drift.

Nevertheless, I have been asked to share and minister at events just down
the road where the cost of living soars, the lawns are manicured to
perfection and the cars are worth, well, a whole lot more than I will make
in a lifetime. However, the people who live there are just the same as
where I live. I even go to Asia twice a year and the folks there are the
same, too. Go figure.

Bottom line: The devil's lies are the same lies everywhere. And, these
lies that we believe about ourselves and about God rob us of true,
satisfying happiness. Only Jesus, the Truth, can rip these *veils* off our
lives. Lord, I'm ready...

What Jesus is whispering to my heart today:

_____

_____

_____

_____

_____

# September 15

I am going to be oh so honest here. Sometimes our circumstances suck.

*But I want you to know, brethren, that the things which happened to me have actually turned out for the furtherance of the gospel,*
Philippians 1:12

Paul most likely wrote this letter during his first Roman imprisonment. Certainly, prison is on no one's *Top Ten* dream destinations. Yet, in this place of being held against his will, Paul introduces us to our God's excessive lavishness to fulfill and satisfy our lives no matter what is taking place and where it is happening. God has a higher plan.

Paul is not calling us to gloss over real, painful, or challenging circumstances. He is calling us to know the Savior intimately by genuinely knowing His presence, His touch, His voice, His strength, and to experience His love in the deepest parts of our being. We can cultivate Christ's presence in our daily lives by simply taking the time to be with Him. And we nurture His healing and delivering power when we learn to experience His Word rather than merely read it.

As we begin to know the Lover of our souls, we will be able to agree with Paul in Philippians 1:18: *In this I rejoice, yes, and will rejoice* because the felt joy of the Lord Jesus has become a reality for us.

What Jesus is whispering to my heart today:

_____

_____

_____

_____

# September 16

We need both scandalous grace and healing truth…

*And the Word became flesh and dwelt among us,*
*and we beheld His glory, the glory as of the only begotten of the Father,*
*full of grace and truth.*
John 1:14

Scandalous grace seems to take so long for each of us to lean into and receive. We have such difficulty forgiving *ourselves* when we fail, so it seems incomprehensible to us that the God of the Universe would extend this lavish gift to us. His grace is a broad place of standing free, complete, and whole in the Father's presence, regardless of what we have done.

And yet, Jesus is healing *Truth*. Truth is sometimes hard to hear or face, yet without it, the lies of our adversary, the devil, will keep us captive. Truth is the healing, delivering, soul-scalpel held by the Great Physician's hand of unending *grace*.

What do you need as you read this? *Grace? Truth?* Jesus is both. Invite Him to speak into your heart in this moment.

What Jesus is whispering to my heart today:

_____

_____

_____

_____

_____

# September 17

*Stay in your own lane!* is a phrase we often hear.

*He said: "I am 'The voice of one crying in the wilderness: "Make straight the way of the LORD," ' as the prophet Isaiah said.*
John 1:23

John the Baptist knew who he was, what he was about, what he was called to do, and he stuck with it. He stayed in his lane and we love him for it – locusts, honey, and all.

I lived too many years wanting be someone else. Wanting to look like someone else, act like someone else, and have the God assignment that someone anyone else had. I wanted to be in any lane but my own. Jesus changed all that.

One of the greatest gifts He has given me is to be comfortable in my own skin. To really enjoy who He has made me to be, even as the goofball I sometimes am. I know what I am supposed to do and I *love* it. I know very few people who can say that about themselves. Only in Jesus, in His presence, can the layers of stuff be driven away and the real you will come forth.

What are you waiting for?

What Jesus is whispering to my heart today:

_____

_____

_____

_____

_____

# September 18

Our family has a sweet home video…

*But the very hairs of your head are all numbered.*
*Do not fear therefore; you are of more value than many sparrows.*
Luke 12:7

Back in the day when our kids were young and video cameras were the size of a refrigerator, my husband captured our six-year old, Jeremy, in a Yellowstone photo-op.

This crazy, funny, and loving towheaded boy was up to his usual antics that, to this day almost 28 years later, still causes our family to roar with laughter. Randy was filming Jeremy dancing around and acting silly directly in front of him. However, Old Faithful Geyser was about to go off and Randy's eyes and heart were fixed upon his child. Finally, Jeremy reached out and nudged the camera toward the miraculous water fountain taking off. *Dad…over here!*

*So remember.* You are the apple of Jesus' eye. He can't take His eyes off of you. Don't let the enemy say it isn't so because nothing could be further from the truth. He is your Father who adores you.

What Jesus is whispering to my heart today:

_____

_____

_____

_____

_____

# September 19

In the midst of this week...

Should the weather be contrary, your kids be raising a ruckus, your job causing chaos, or you just plain 'ole don't want to face another week, realize you have lost His joy somewhere. Jesus tells us our joy can't be taken away from us, yet somehow you have given it away. Hmmm. Beat it back into His presence *asap*. In His presence is *fullness of joy*. *Psalm 16:11*

Should you be struggling with a relationship, a financial hardship, or a shipwreck in your life, it is time to draw under the feather of His wings and power. Take a look at *Psalm 91*. Read it slowly. What is He saying to you? Listen. Draw even closer.

This is a week of new beginnings, hopes to be realized, and miracles to watch for. Keep your eyes open, your heart tender, and your mind from distraction. This week will be awesome in Jesus because He Who is in you is greater than anything! *1 John 4:4*

What Jesus is whispering to my heart today:

_____

_____

_____

_____

_____

# September 20

These words are for us...

*Jesus said to him, "If I will that he remain till I come, what is that to you? You follow Me."*
John 21:22

In other words – *quit comparing!*

For years I compared myself with others. I was either hoping that I could be like someone I saw or silently rejoicing that I wasn't similar to someone else. What *poison* comparison was to my soul!

I have learned the hard way. The only thing I need to focus on is what Jesus is doing in my life and follow closely behind Him. It is foolhardy to look to the right or the left of any path He leads me on. It is even more disastrous when I try to take someone else's path that He didn't give me. This is true discipleship. This is true communion with Christ.

Take it from me, a former *comparer-extraordinaire*. There is no better way to live than to have Jesus be the only One you measure your life with – the only One you want to emulate and follow.

What Jesus is whispering to my heart today:

_____

_____

_____

_____

_____

# September 21

I have a heroine found on the pages of the New Testament...

*Now there was one, Anna...She was of a great age...and this woman was a widow of about eighty-four years, who did not depart from the temple, but served God with fastings and prayers night and day.*
Luke 2:36-37

Though there is much to say about Anna. Still, what speaks to me from her story is that she could have missed her divine appointment with the Christ child. She could have decided to sleep in, chit-chat with Hannah down the road, or linger at the market for fresh donuts and a latte. She could have easily missed the greatest moment of her life!

Nevertheless, she didn't miss this extraordinary encounter with Jesus. She lived *sold out* for and totally in love with God. She was faithful to the ministry He had called her to – even when no one probably noticed or knew her name. And it sure sounds like she knew Him intimately, letting Him direct her path throughout the day

So, let's be like Anna. Because if we are faithful and obedient to the Lord in the *little things*, we will be in the *right place at the right time* for His really *big things*. Enough said.

What Jesus is whispering to my heart today:

_____

_____

_____

_____

_____

# September 22

One of my favorite *photographs* from all four Gospels...

*So they all ate and were filled. And they took up twelve baskets full of fragments and of the fish.*
Mark 6:42-43

Wow. *Jesus took so little and made so much.* This speaks to every area of our lives. Where do you feel small and insufficient? Is it your life, your resources, your future, your hopes – yourself? Place it in His hands and stand back to watch the wonder. Just like the bread, He may need to break up a few things in your life to bring growth, but do not fear His tender touch.

*Everyone was fille*d. I spent much of my Christian life unsatisfied and frustrated. Ministry was more chore than overflow. The lack of knowing God's will for my life was the norm, and I struggled with habitual, destructive behaviors until Jesus cornered me. In *Him alone* am I satisfied, significant, and complete.

Finally, He doesn't waste a thing. Only Jesus can take the junk of our past and turn it into gold. He turns our waste into our miraculous story in Him. So, take a few moments and talk to the Lord Jesus about all of this. He's ready to begin a miracle in you.

What Jesus is whispering to my heart today:

_____

_____

_____

_____

_____

# September 23

Surrender. Really. This one word says it all.

*You will show me the path of life; In Your presence is fullness of joy; At Your right hand are pleasures forevermore.*
Psalm 16:11

You see, God is crazy in love with each and every one of us. Even those of us who aren't crazy in love with Him. Nevertheless, there is a caveat – surrender. He wants *all* of us – no part of our being held in reserve – He wants everything. Sooner, rather than later!

The verses leading up to this marvelous passage tell us – the Lord *has to be* our *portion*. He has to be our *everything*. We are told that we must implicitly *trust* Him, *seek* His counsel, and keep Him as the *ultimate priority* in our lives. Jesus first – everything else takes a back seat.

Have you noticed our joy quotient is directly related to our *surrender*? So what are we waiting for? Let's walk His path of life. Let's experience the bliss of His presence regardless of what we're going through and let's thoroughly enjoy His daily pleasure for His Kingdom, His Cause, and for those who don't know Him yet. They need to see the real deal.

Ahhhh, yes. *Surrender*. The only way to live.

What Jesus is whispering to my heart today:

_____

_____

_____

_____

_____

# September 24

Bummer. You know, some prayer battles are long and arduous...

*Now there was a long war between the house of Saul and the house of David. But David grew stronger and stronger, and the house of Saul grew weaker and weaker.*
2 Samuel 3:1

Sometimes, we are praying to our Father when He has told us that He has *given us* authority in His name to smite the enemy's advances. But we keep praying for *Him* to do something, and He is waiting for us!

Many times, the battle rages long because there are many components to the coming answer. There are other lives and circumstances God is lining up before the puzzle pieces can come together. Yet, we grow impatient and try to take matters into our own hands. Don't do that!

When the prayer battle lingers, ask the Lord for direction regarding *how* to pray and *what* demonic strongholds you need to break in His name. Fast when you are called to fast and ask for specific scriptures to hold onto and stand on. You may be in for a long haul, so *pace* yourself: pray fervently when prompted to, but rest in-between times. Hang tough, keeping your eyes ever on your Faithful Commander. He will answer your prayer.

What Jesus is whispering to my heart today:

_____

_____

_____

_____

_____

# September 25

There are many Bible accounts that trigger my imagination…

*And it shall be, when you hear the sound of marching in the tops of the mulberry trees, then you shall advance quickly. For then the LORD will go out before you to strike the camp of the Philistines.*
2 Samuel 5:24

Today a friend and I were both commenting how desperately we want to see the release of more heaven on earth through the Spirit's power to heal, save, and deliver in every aspect of human existence. As I went for a short walk through the eucalyptus trees that frame the island we live on the wind was singing through the treetops and the Spirit was ministering to my soul.

*Now is the time.* We have had plenty of teaching (though we must always remain teachable and hungry for the authentic teaching of God's Word). We must understand we will *never* feel ready, for if we did, we wouldn't rely completely upon Him. And, we can't wait until it is *comfortable.*

It is time to *believe* what we know. Rather, *believe Who* we know. Let's not be afraid to walk in the power of His Word and the nine gifts of the Spirit, nor be timid to seize back lives from the adversary. The Lord is with us and it is the hour of breakthrough, just as it was for David.

What Jesus is whispering to my heart today:

_____

_____

_____

_____

_____

# September 26

In the midst of this week...

Should life seem daunting at work, in school, or with family, Jesus tells us to take one day at a time. Listen to this instruction! *His* constant grace and power will be more than enough to meet your daily demands as you lean wholly into Him.
*Matthew 6:34*

Should you find yourself feeling weak, about to cave, and you can't take another step forward, let Him carry you. Find Jesus beside the *still waters* of time spent with Him. Think of all the things you have to be grateful for and let Jesus' joy flood your soul and spirit. The joy of the Lord is your strength, not your bank account, your friends, or your good looks. Okay, I had to throw that in there for fun!
*Psalm 23:2*

This is a week of new beginnings, hopes to be realized, and miracles to watch for. Keep your eyes open, your heart tender, and your mind from distraction. This week will be awesome in Jesus because He Who is in you is greater than anything!
*1 John 4:4*

What Jesus is whispering to my heart today:

_____

_____

_____

_____

_____

# September 27

Have you ever come to the end of your rope?

*And when they ran out of wine,*
*the mother of Jesus said to Him, "They have no wine."*
John 2:3

Have you ever run out of...*yourself*? No more left to give, no more options, no more fixes, and no more resources? Have you ever run out of hope?

We all have. And truthfully, Jesus often waits for us to come to the end of ourselves so we won't settle for less than His very best for us. Certainly, He knew the wine was running low, but He waited. He waited to be asked to intervene.

And He waits for us.

But why wait until we have exhausted ourselves – until our ideas and our trying to control people and circumstances come crashing down? Let's give Jesus all our stuff *now*. Hands off completely and let Him call the plays in His own timing.

Let's invite Him to turn the water of our lives into exquisite wine.

What Jesus is whispering to my heart today:

_____

_____

_____

_____

_____

# September 28

Secretly, I love presents…

*For out of His fullness (abundance) we have all received [all had a share and we were all supplied with] one grace after another and spiritual blessing upon spiritual blessing and even favor upon favor and gift [heaped] upon gift.*
John 1:16 AMP

I know it is more blessed to give than to receive, nevertheless, I honestly love receiving gifts on my birthday or holidays. Yet I struggle when Jesus *is* the One giving them to me.

I often leave His gifts wrapped in their boxes with the pretty ribbons left untied. So beautiful to gaze upon, but I'm not sure I am worthy, ready, or willing to open His gifts. Yet, He pursues me and never gives up on me until I someday open these gifts and make them mine. He wants me to tear into these presents with abandon like a toddler on their birthday.

He paid the highest price to purchase these incomparable gifts for us. I don't want to let these wonder-filled treasures go unopened any longer. How about you?

What Jesus is whispering to my heart today:

_____

_____

_____

_____

_____

# September 29

There is something special about mornings…

*Every morning you'll hear me at it again.*
*Every morning I lay out the pieces of my life on your altar*
*and watch for fire to descend.*
Psalm 105:3 MSG

I get it that some of us don't even know which way is up until we have had our third cup of coffee. Nevertheless, starting our day by laying everything about our lives on God's altar can be the catalyst for all He wants to do throughout the day.

Just a few quiet moments with our Maker...

*To settle our minds,*
*To pour out our hearts,*
*To surrender our lives,*
*To experience the wonder of His presence,*
*To hear His voice,*
*To let Him consume us until all that remains is Him.*

We can't live well without this launching pad. It will make all the difference in the rest of our day and the rest of our lives.

What Jesus is whispering to my heart today:

_____

_____

_____

_____

_____

# September 30

These wonderful words...

*Be still, and know that I am God;*
*I will be exalted among the nations,*
*I will be exalted in the earth!*
Psalm 46:10

For us to genuinely know our Creator intimately, we must have moments of complete and utter *stillness*. Being still is one of the most challenging things for us to do! Really. Even when we calm our body, our heart and mind generally keep racing. Right?

Nevertheless, solitude and quiet are a cultivated and most necessary joy.

God is telling us that we will truly begin to *know* Him when we are still; when we are quiet. Not with our laundry list of prayers or questions. Not with a crowd of others that may distract. But alone with Him – our mind silent and our heart hushed with expectancy. He has been waiting for us to come and enjoy His company.

This verse is more than a beautiful quote. It is an invitation from the heart of God to come and know Him as the Lover of our souls.

What Jesus is whispering to my heart today:

_____

_____

_____

_____

_____

# October 1

Have you ever felt like your life was tied up in *knots*?

*... For this purpose the Son of God was manifested,*
*that He might destroy the works of the devil.*
1 John 3:8

Mine sure was. Yes, my life was in a million knots. Truly a hot mess.
But Jesus came to rescue me. And you.

The original language for the word *destroy* in the verse above means to
*loosen, let go,* and *set free from.* Jesus came to loosen every knot of our
own doing, our own sin, and the mess of our family's generational past.
He can untie the knots of the enemy that have caused us hurt, heartache,
and tragedy.

Some of us are so knotted up that it seems impossible we will ever be
free. We doubt, give up, and give in...to our knots. But Jesus can free us.
Yes, really. I am still a work in progress, but I am not the person I once
was. Freedom is indescribable-beyond-description, wonder and joy.

What are you waiting for? Invite Him to untie your knots one at a time.
He is able and He is willing.

What Jesus is whispering to my heart today:

_____

_____

_____

_____

_____

# October 2

It started as a goofy thing, my nick-name *Sue Bee*...

*Awake, awake, Deborah! Awake, awake, sing a song!*
*Arise...lead your captives away...*
Judges 5:12

I was working at a ginormous county office and I started signing all of
my emails as *Sue Bee*. Get it? Sue Bee, Sue B, Sue Boldt. Silly, huh?

Nevertheless, God works in amazing ways. Years later, while reading the
story of Israel's judge Deborah *Judges 4-5,* I heard His still, small voice
telling me, I am a *Deborah.* One who is not only in the midst of battle,
but training others to wage war and see the enemy vanquished. I hope
this doesn't sound pretentious, but Jesus was confirming again what He
had already spoken over my life, what He had impassioned me for,
designed me for, and equipped me for.

And then I read my Bible's notes. The meaning of the name, *Deborah* is
*honey bee.* My nick-name was prophetic.

All this to say, He has a name and a calling, for you. If you aren't sure of
it yet, look for the little things He is doing and saying around you. Lean
into His presence. He will make it all clear.

What Jesus is whispering to my heart today:

_____

_____

_____

_____

_____

# October 3

In the midst of this week...

Should you find yourself up against overwhelming circumstances, trust them into the care of the One who is greater than anything you can face. Next, wait quietly for what He might have you do or *not do* in your situation. He holds you close and you don't have to walk this way alone.
*Hebrews 13:5*

If your health, finances, or future are in question – it is time to turn to His Word. What does *He* say about your situation? He will make a way through the wilderness, but it needs to be *His* way, not yours.
*Isaiah 43:20*

This is a week of new beginnings, hopes to be realized, and miracles to watch for. Keep your eyes open, your heart tender, and your mind from distraction. This week will be awesome in Jesus because He Who is in you is greater than anything!
*1 John 4:4*

What Jesus is whispering to my heart today:

_____

_____

_____

_____

_____

# October 4

You are qualified...

*Giving thanks to the Father who has qualified us to be*
*partakers of the inheritance of the saints in the light.*
Colossians 1:12

I think this is one of the most challenging truths to drum through our heads. Especially me. I have felt so disqualified from all my inheritance in Jesus because of my past. My past failure, rebellion, sin, and just plain doing some truly foolish things.

How about you?

Do you feel the same way at times? Yet, God's word trumps our failures. His anguish on the cross secured our qualification. Our sins are forgiven, as this passage goes on to tell us. This is the truth – His truth, and who are we to argue? And this truth is our launching pad – what we couldn't do, He did.

It is time to start living in this truth and doing what the Holy Spirit is placing in our hearts to accomplish for Jesus' Kingdom. He has already *qualified us* for the task at hand.

What Jesus is whispering to my heart today:

_____

_____

_____

_____

_____

# October 5

Have you ever heard the words, "Don't leave home without it??"

*And being assembled together with them, He commanded them not to depart from Jerusalem, but to wait for the Promise of the Father, "Which," He said, "you have heard from Me."*
Acts 1:4

In this case, the phrase doesn't refer to a thing. Instead, Jesus is referring to the Person and power of the Holy Spirit. He is telling the disciples, "*Yes, there is more.*" The *more* is the day of Pentecost when Holy Spirit fire fell, birthing the early church, and the gospel spread like wildfire.

The Holy Spirit is for today as well. We need His power more than ever in this day and age. We need to cultivate all of His fruit, such as love, joy, peace, but we also need His giftings of miracles, spiritual language, and discerning of spirits, to name a few (see 1 Cor. 12)

So, do you need His *more* in your life? Do you need a refreshing infilling of His presence? The Father is waiting for your simple, heartfelt request. Take a look at His promise for you in Luke 11:11-13. Come and be filled, and don't leave home without Him.

What Jesus is whispering to my heart today:

_____

_____

_____

_____

_____

# October 6

We should never give up our pursuit of total freedom from our stuff; our soul stuff that keeps us from an over-the-top, extraordinary life in Christ.

*To console those who mourn in Zion,*
*To give them beauty for ashes, The oil of joy for mourning,*
*The garment of praise for the spirit of heaviness...*
Isaiah 61:3a

What do you hope for from this list? Make it your prayer today and write it down in a journal. Be open to how the Holy Spirit will break the enemy's lies to you – that Jesus tells us is the root of all bondage.

Freedom may come in a minute or it may come more slowly as Jesus walks you gently, but firmly forward, one step at a time. Don't settle for just getting by or coping. Contend for His breakthrough in your life for:

*Beauty*
*Joy*
*Praise*
*Righteousness*

Please think and pray about these things...today.

What Jesus is whispering to my heart today:

_____

_____

_____

_____

_____

# October 7

The thing about daily life is: it is just so *daily*…

*…and the cares of this world, the deceitfulness of riches,*
*and the desires for other things entering in choke the word, and it*
*becomes unfruitful.*
Mark 4:19

The well-known daily life quote above easily pertains to this verse. The daily struggles of family, finances, work, homework, you name it. They often drown out our passion for Jesus, His Word, and His power.

Our weekly workplace Bible Study members talked about this today. Honestly. Just the everyday stuff of living can chip away at us. I know it often dulls my senses to the things of the Spirit. Yet, we made an agreement today. A bunch of us are holding each other accountable to be expectant of the Spirit's miraculous working every day in our midst. Ten minutes after making this decision, I had the opportunity to pray for healing from cancer for someone who sauntered into my office looking for a phone number.

So I'm in. No more daily dullness, but Holy Spirit fullness instead. Want to join with us?

What Jesus is whispering to my heart today:

_____

_____

_____

_____

_____

# October 8

Almost all of us have some form of desolation from our family tree...

*And they shall rebuild the old ruins,*
*They shall raise up the former desolations,*
*And they shall repair the ruined cities,*
*The desolations of many generations.*
Isaiah 61:4

This verse speaks directly to our past in regard to our family: our family history, environment, and the circumstances we were raised in. Personally, I grew up in a loving home, but it wasn't until years later that I realized how dysfunctional it was. I needed some deep healing.

How about you? Addiction, divorce, sexual ruin, rage, compulsiveness, bitterness, self-pity, sickness, and the list goes on. These are issues we disdain, yet are oh so familiar marks of our families; of ourselves.

Nevertheless, the word *shall,* from this passage, triumphs. As we pursue Jesus – He *shall* and He *will* bring us out of the ruins of our family's past. He will repair us completely as we invite Him into these closets. Let's open the door and not be afraid of His tender touch to deliver us from these desolations. He shall do it.

What Jesus is whispering to my heart today:

_____

_____

_____

_____

_____

# October 9

We all need food to survive, thrive, and truly live...

*Jesus said to them, "My food is to do the will of Him who sent Me, and to finish His work."*
John 4:34

I've been pondering this verse during my quiet time with Jesus on this last day in Taiwan ministering with Youth With a Mission (YWAM). Soon, I'll be heading home to start new adventures in Him there.

The Spirit is calling me deeper. He is calling me to deeper *surrender*. I want to spend the remaining years of my life only fulfilling Christ's agenda, His plan, and His purpose for me. Honestly, He has already fulfilled every dream I ever had for myself, better than I could have ever expected. I just want to go out in a blaze of glory, *His glory*. Bring it on, Lord!

This is my food, my nourishment: finishing the work He created me for. Want to join me?

I know it will be a thrill ride!

What Jesus is whispering to my heart today:

_____

_____

_____

_____

_____

# October 10

In the midst of this week...

Should you be feeling forlorn, forgotten, or you are in a fog of confusion – it is time to break free and have a breakthrough with Jesus. Your portion in Christ is fullness of joy, hope, life, and a future. Spend some time with the Savior in fresh surrender, lay down your plans for His, and get a brand new word from His Word. Jesus is faithful.
*Romans 14:17*

Should you be exhausted, edgy, eating too much, spending too much, or you are just plainly in a downward spiral, it is time to look up! Your Redeemer is closer than your next breath. Ask the Holy Spirit to fill your tank to overflowing and remember His gifts found in *1 Corinthians 12:8-10*. Don't leave home without them.

This is a week of new beginnings, hopes to be realized, and miracles to watch for. Keep your eyes open, your heart tender, and your mind from distraction. This week will be awesome in Jesus because He Who is in you is greater than anything!
*1 John 4:4*

What Jesus is whispering to my heart today:

_____

_____

_____

_____

# October 11

I realize I write about this frequently. Possibly, it is because I need to remind myself so often. Be still...

*Be still, and know that I am God;*
*I will be exalted among the nations,*
*I will be exalted in the earth!*
*The LORD of hosts is with us; The God of Jacob is our refuge." Selah*
Psalm 46:10-11

There is no substitute for quiet and solitude in the presence of the Almighty. It is the oxygen of our soul and spirit; the bread of life for our thoughts and emotions, the living water of God's clear and sound thinking, and the raw emotion of His touch.

We long for it and don't even know it. Personally, I can search for it in all the wrong places and always come up empty until I simply come, kneel down before Him, and receive Jesus' touch in the quiet...

Quiet. Stillness. No worship band. No sermon download. No social media upload. No one else but God and myself. He is always more than enough for whatever I need in any given moment. Always. Forever.

What Jesus is whispering to my heart today:

_____

_____

_____

_____

_____

# October 12

We just started our day with prayer at my workplace…

*So He said to them, "When you pray, say: Our Father in heaven, Hallowed be Your name. Your kingdom come. Your will be done On earth as it is in heaven."*
Luke 11:2

I opened my eyes as Jaime prayed powerful words, bringing heaven down in the hallways, offices, and waiting rooms of the medical clinic where we work.

I looked down and saw four pairs of shoes forming our prayer huddle. I didn't see any Manalo Blahnik shoes in the pack. I also didn't see any other high-end heels or anything termed fancy. Nope. I was aware of tennis shoes, booties, and two pairs of flats, slightly worn. Nobody in this prayer team with celebrity status or big bucks in the bank – just humble, passionate women filled with faith.

Yet, heaven was poured out. The Holy Spirit was invited to bring healing and conviction in every room in this place. The atmosphere changed all because we took the time to pray, *Your kingdom come, now, Lord!*

What Jesus is whispering to my heart today:

_____

_____

_____

_____

_____

# October 13

What is the name of endearment Jesus has given you?

*...You shall be called by a new name,*
*Which the mouth of the LORD will name.*
Isaiah 62:2b

No, I'm not into any off-the-wall-new-name cult, yet there are several Scriptures which tell us that He will speak a new name over us when we see Him face-to-face. Yet, what does He name us *now*?

Jesus first called John, and his brother James, *Sons of Thunder!* Remember, they were the crew who wanted to incinerate some folks who weren't open to the Lord's message.

Yet, just like John, a person cannot be in Jesus' presence long without experiencing His transforming touch. John, as an eye-witness to the Majesty of God, once named a *Son of Thunder* became the *Beloved Disciple*. And this same John, who once had wanted fire to fall, penned the most famous phrase in history...

*For God so loved the world...*

I encourage you to ask Jesus to tell you the name He has for you. He will and you will be changed just by hearing His voice whisper it in your ear.

What Jesus is whispering to my heart today:

_____

_____

_____

_____

_____

# October 14

I want to be on God's *Special Ops* team...

*Then David again gathered all the elite troops in Israel, 30,000 in all.*
2 Samuel 6:1 NLT

I am pretty sure David's elite crew were the fastest, the strongest, and the bravest. However, I am not so sure that Jesus' team has to have those qualifications.

His elite team players only have one requirement: Love, love, and more love.

Love – sold-out, life-altering love for Him first. That doesn't mean you or I have to be the best or the brightest. Instead, we just need to live solely for Him. Hunger for His presence is our training and healing ground. We need to be skillful in His Word to defeat our adversary and speak life to others. However, it is our love for everyone that is our badge of courage. If we are fully engaged in His wondrous love – knowing He will take care of our every need – we have no fear that when we give ourselves or our resources away, He will replenish us to overflowing.

All I can say is, sign me up, Lord, for your Special Ops team!

What Jesus is whispering to my heart today:

_____

_____

_____

_____

_____

# October 15

To fear the Lord means to really know *Who* He is...

*How great is the goodness*
*You have stored up for those who fear You,*
*You lavish it on those who come to You for protection,*
*Blessing them before the watching world.*
Psalm 31:19 NLT

We serve God Almighty; the awesome and fearsome Sovereign and the Creator of *all* that is. The One Whom the Bible tells us owns our breath in His hands and owns all of our ways is the God of wonder, creativity, wisdom, righteousness, and holiness.

Yet, He is our is Abba-Daddy – for those of us who have received Him. When we run to Him for protection, for His covering, and His relentless love, oh what joy it brings to His heart.

Nope. No worry, anxiety, or care can be found in His arms when we tuck ourselves safely into them. It is a good indicator of when we are *not* in this special embrace if we *are* filled with worry, anxiety, or care.

The promise is lavish, but the condition must be met. Read the verse again, then run to shelter in the refuge of the One and Only.

What Jesus is whispering to my heart today:

_____

_____

_____

_____

_____

# October 16

Only our Creator knows what will fill our sails...

*The lines have fallen to me in pleasant places;*
*Yes, I have a good inheritance.*
Psalm 16:6

This verse speaks of the boundaries of our inheritance in Christ. Ask yourself these questions: Who are you really? What Jesus is doing in you? What causes your heart to sing, and what are your passions and dreams?

I spent years wishing I had someone else's boundaries; their inheritance. I had fallen into the sin Adam and Eve fell for thinking that God was holding out on me. The last few years have been the awakening of my soul to all He HAS given me – in me, through me, and what He will do in the future. It wasn't until I found His bliss in the life He had given me, that my boundaries started to grow larger, sweeter, and deeper than I could have imagined.

Are you discontent about your life? Go to the Creator. Let Him call the plays and let Him change the paradigm of your thinking. Life in Him begins when this takes place.

What Jesus is whispering to my heart today:

_____

_____

_____

_____

_____

# October 17

In the midst of this week...

If you already feel ambushed by life, circumstances, or possibly you may even feel ambushed by the people around you, look to the Lord Jesus! Take as much time as you need in His presence to restore your weary soul. Nothing else will do. Ask Him for a specific Scripture for your situation that you can hang onto. He will give it to you.
*Ephesians 6:17*

If your gas tank is empty, your bank account down the tubes, and your joy level scraping the bottom, turn to the One who loves and knows you best. Ask for His direction – then do it. Enough said.
*James 1:5*

This is a week of new beginnings, hopes to be realized, and miracles to watch for. Keep your eyes open, your heart tender, and your mind from distraction. This week will be awesome in Jesus because He Who is in you is greater than anything!
*1 John 4:4*

What Jesus is whispering to my heart today:

_____

_____

_____

_____

_____

# October 18

If it doesn't matter to me, it doesn't matter.

*For because you did not do it the first time, the LORD our God broke out against us, because we did not consult Him about the proper order.*
1 Chronicles 15:13

I have found this selfish attitude in myself and I've seen it lately in others. Not good. If something doesn't matter, isn't important, or of concern to me, I can be pretty cavalier and insensitive to some very important things. Apparently, King David had the same issue at times.

David's disregard for the Lord's instruction about moving the holy articles of the tabernacle cost a man's life. Israel actually lost God's presence in their midst for a period of time, just because of simple disregard. Of course we can get legalistic about dotting every "i" and crossing every "t." Nope. This isn't what I am addressing.

We need to be careful not to be *careless* about what is important to others and to the Lord. Our witness is often at risk because we disregard rules or requests that get in our way at home, work, school, or anywhere. I am talking about the little things we face every day. God has greater purposes for us and a lot of it is His integrity in our lives. And this matters to Him very much.

What Jesus is whispering to my heart today:

_____

_____

_____

_____

_____

# October 19

Do you want to become well?

*When Jesus noticed him lying there helpless...He said to him, "Do you want to become well: Are you really in earnest about getting well?"*
John 5:6 AMPC

Sure, I want to get well! Jesus seems to ask a rhetorical question here, but maybe He isn't. As the Amplified Bible states here, are we truly earnest about His healing touch?

Thinking over several years of my life, I honestly question if I genuinely desired to be made well in my soul. I liked my stuff and my issues more than I liked the thought of being free. Would the Holy Spirit be enough to satisfy? That is laughable and tragic all at the same time. Yet, I was destroying myself, my walk with the Lord, and hurting my family.

Self-pity. That can be the culprit of us not letting the Holy Spirit dig deep in us to set us free. We are comfortable in this zip code even if it looks and feels like hell. Nevertheless, freedom is oh so worth whatever we may have to face to get there. Jesus will walk us through it all to real living.

Yes, Lord. I want to become well.

What Jesus is whispering to my heart today:

_____
_____
_____
_____
_____

# October 20

Hang with me here.

Say a quick prayer asking the Holy Spirit to speak from His Heart to yours. Now, read this passage slowly...

*...For He, God Himself has said, "I will not in any way fail you nor give you up nor leave you without support.*
*I will not,*
*I will not,*
*I will not*
*in any degree leave you helpless nor forsake nor let you down relax My hold on you! Assuredly not!"*
Hebrews 13:5b AMPC

Ponder what He is speaking directly to your heart. Maybe write this verse out for yourself and underline what He is saying.

Please take the time to read Hebrews 13:5 in its entirety, for the context of it tells us clearly that Jesus is all we need. He is all sufficient and all satisfying. Come to Him now and surrender more of yourself to Him – I will too! Yes, He is all we need in whatever we are facing. He will not let go of us.

What Jesus is whispering to my heart today:

_____

_____

_____

_____

_____

# October 21

It's never about others. Jesus is after us...

*Examine yourselves to see whether you are in the faith; test yourselves…*
2 Corinthians 13:5

It is so easy to look to others as the reason for our unhappiness, our dissatisfaction, or our stuff. *If only* – we think about those close to us. *If only – they were different.* We pray and pray for the folks in our lives to change, but God doesn't seem to answer our prayers. So, we remain stuck. Stuck in *our* lives.

Does this resonate with you in any way? Have you ever had these thoughts? Been there, done that myself. Yet, it wasn't until I let Jesus ruthlessly speak into *my* life about *my* stuff, *my* selfishness, and *my* issues did radical transformation happen in me and around me.

Someone needs to hear this. You are blaming others, yet King Jesus is after you. Nothing is going to change around you until you let Him deal with you first. Stop playing the blame game because healing and restoration begin with *you*. Let Him clean your house and then see the bounty of His abundant life explode around you.

What Jesus is whispering to my heart today:

_____

_____

_____

_____

_____

# October 22

Paul speaks to us through the ages about extraordinary joy...

*Rejoice in the Lord always. Again I will say, rejoice!*
Philippians 4:4

This overwhelming joy is real, palpable, and can be experienced in every moment of life regardless of circumstances. God's joy is not merely a good theory, a nice sentiment or a quote, but it is tangible and available to every person who proclaims Jesus is Lord of their life.

Paul is extending this invitation to abundant joy from the confines of a dungeon cell with the possibility of facing imminent execution. Yet he *is* overwhelmed with the Holy Spirit's comfort, peace, contentment, and yes, happiness. And this is the power of his testimony: he is experiencing beyond-reason joy *in the midst of* stress, trial, and danger. If he can know this amazing emotion in the midst of his daunting circumstances, he shares that *we can, too.*

What are you facing in your life's circumstances today? Relational or financial loss? Possibly health trauma, family drama, or purposelessness? Divorce, separation, or death? Paul points the way for us to live beyond what we could imagine or think – the extraordinary joy of the Lord Jesus.

What Jesus is whispering to my heart today:

_____

_____

_____

_____

_____

# October 23

We live in a day where celebrity and fame are everything...

*Therefore when Jesus perceived that they were about to come and take Him by force to make Him king, He departed again to the mountain by Himself alone.*
John 6:15

Honestly. Our culture is *nutsie-cuckoo* when it comes to anyone whose name is *known*. We strive for it ourselves. Or at least I did, even if it was by living in a fantasy world of my own making. How many likes or followers do we have in social media, at work, at home, or in life? We can come under the delusion that our worth depends upon these things. We live wrong-side up.

Not Jesus, however. Walking earth as a man, dependent upon the Father, He knew where His fame and worth were derived. Alone with the Father is where He went. Fully God, He also draws us to Himself. He knows that we will only know our full potential and our full worth in His fame alone.

Let's live this day right-side up. We are fully known and loved by Him and that is more than our hearts could ever desire. Walk in the joy of this truth.

What Jesus is whispering to my heart today:

_____

_____

_____

_____

_____

# October 24

In the midst of this week...

Should your yard be overgrown, your jeans too tight, or your wallet a little too empty, look up! King Jesus is the All-Sufficient One. Set your eyes on Him alone and let Him do the heavy lifting for your cares.
*Philippians 4:19*

Should a loved one go sideways, a neighbor goes ballistic, or a co-worker becomes annoying, well, remember you have issues, too! Jesus has all the patience in the world to bring you into freedom. Now, grab hold of His patience in you for others, by the power of the Holy Spirit!
*Galatians 5:22-23*

This is a week of new beginnings, hopes to be realized, and miracles to watch for. Keep your eyes open, your heart tender, and your mind from distraction. This week will be awesome in Jesus because He Who is in you is greater than anything!
*1 John 4:4*

Feel free to share...

What Jesus is whispering to my heart today:

_____

_____

_____

_____

_____

# October 27

Am I the only person who has a hard time focusing?

*Let your eyes look straight ahead,*
*And your eyelids look right before you.*
Proverbs 4:25

Similar passages are found throughout the Bible, so I think the Lord is trying to get a point across to us, especially in this day and age when there is so much to take us off His course. I get distracted from one room to the next in my own home – a million things to think about or do just in the ten steps that I take.

Our walk of faith requires focus. What is He working on in your life right now? Here is a simple tip from the master-of-life-bondages, namely me...

Focus on one aspect of healing and deliverance in your life at a time. Get that *one thing* beat before you move on to the next area. Don't get caught in the swamp of not seeking Jesus' intervention in your life because you have too much stuff to be free from. Take it one step at a time and focus on Him to guide you to breakthrough.

He will.

What Jesus is whispering to my heart today:

_____

_____

_____

_____

_____

# October 28

Are you compulsive or impulsive? You don't have to be...

*Ponder the path of your feet*
*And let all your ways be established.*
Proverbs 4:26

As neuroscientist, Dr. Caroline Leaf, would say, science is now catching up with what the Bible has said all along. Our brains and our thought-lives can truly be rewired by the power of the Holy Spirit. Simply check out *Romans 12:1-2* to see this is so.

Ponder what you are doing next. If being compulsive or impulsive is a problem for you – I was the latter of these two – take the time today to stop and think before you act or speak. Seemingly impossible at first, and cumbersome too. Nevertheless, it is imperative for us check, and often stop, our actions so that we might start hearing the Holy Spirit speak into our everyday situations. These two behaviors are simply lies about ourselves from the enemy. You and I were not meant to live this way.

So, do this for the Lord: Every day for a week, starting today or tomorrow morning, ponder, wait, consider, and slow down before you do *anything*. Simplistic, but it is a Biblical start to walking in the Spirit.

What Jesus is whispering to my heart today:

_____

_____

_____

_____

_____

# October 29

The story of Jesus feeding the multitudes is a picture of grace...

*There is a lad here who has five barley loaves and two small fish,*
*But what are they among so many?*
John 6:9

First, Jesus takes the little to nothing of our lives that we bring to Him and He multiplies it exponentially because of His thanks to the Father that we have come. Really. That seems like it should be the other way around. We need to be the ones who continually give thanksgiving.

Next, He increases our lives beyond the scope of our imagination. Yes, we can miss this part by trying to take back control of our own destiny. I sidelined myself for years. My advice? Don't take back control. Total surrender is the way to go.

Finally, Jesus even uses the waste of our lives to bring Himself glory. So don't discount anything as disqualifying you from His purposes, because you know what I think happened to those leftovers on that miraculous feast day? I think people took them home to feed their friends and families the miracle they had experienced.

Yes. This is a story of God's amazing grace.

What Jesus is whispering to my heart today:

_____

_____

_____

_____

_____

# October 30

My oldest daughter, well, she gave her dad and I some anxious days and some sleepless nights during a few of her teenaged years...

*...being confident of this very thing, that He who has begun a good work in you will complete it until the day of Jesus Christ.*
Philippians 1:6

The drama of youthful angst, messy bedrooms, goofy girlfriends, some not so desirable boyfriends, and a dash of attitude kept us on our knees in prayer for her. Yet, did we ever give up on Dayspring Melissa? No, never. Did we want to throw in the towel, move away, and not leave a forwarding address for her? Jesus never gives up on us, either.

This confidence is based upon Jesus Himself. Jesus, who began this excellent work in us is the basis of this overwhelming hope. His plans do not rely upon our frailty and failings, but upon the His Holy Spirit working in and through us. We only need to have open and ready hearts to receive His touch to complete what He has started.

You know, my daughter's name is written in my Bible at this verse – written during one of those sleepless nights. And, as I witness the amazing, beautiful Jesus-follower she is today, God isn't failing us or her. The same will be true for you and me as well.

What Jesus is whispering to my heart today:

_____

_____

_____

_____

_____

# October 31

In the midst of this week...

Should the events of the day in our nation and around the world rock us
to our core, this is when the Comfort of the Holy Spirit surrounds us. Ask
for a fresh infilling of His presence to drive fear and anxiety from your
soul. He is our peace in any storm.
*2 Timothy 1:7*

Should the world seem darker and more desperate, we are seeing exactly
what King Jesus told us would happen. It is time for us to be sold-out for
His Kingdom. We need to stand completely upon His Word, knowing it
for ourselves. We need to learn to be comfortable walking in all nine
gifts of the Holy Spirit which are necessary for this day.
*Matthew 24:1-31*

This is a week of new beginnings, hopes to be realized, and miracles to
watch for. Keep your eyes open, your heart tender, and your mind from
distraction. This week will be awesome in Jesus because He Who is in
you is greater than anything!
*1 John 4:4*

What Jesus is whispering to my heart today:

_____

_____

_____

_____

_____

# November 1

Even if this is not your belief or practice, please prayerfully consider and study God's Word to discover that the gift of speaking in tongues, or spiritual language, is for every believer...

*He who speaks in a tongue edifies himself,*
*But he who prophecies edifies the church.*
1 Corinthians 14:4

Without a lengthy teaching here, this gift of the Spirit is the beyond-belief biggest aid to your walk in Christ, your Bible reading, your steps in the miraculous, and for personal breakthrough. The Holy Spirit praying through you – a dedicated avenue to the Father's throne.

It is this easy to receive: Ask the Holy Spirit to fill you to overflowing. This is known as the Baptism in the Holy Spirit, *John 1:33, Acts 2.* As you focus your attention on Jesus, begin speaking ***out loud*** any syllables that are not English or another language you may know. As you take this step of faith, the Spirit will gently take over your speech. You will be able to stop and start your new prayer language at any time. At first it may seem rather slow and halting, or crazy-fast! You may be tempted to think that you are making up the words, but don't get discouraged. Keep yielding to the Spirit and He will increase your spiritual vocabulary.

Pray in the Spirit continually. It is a fountain of encouragement, breakthrough, and power for your life and Jesus wants you to have it and use it. That simple.

What Jesus is whispering to my heart today:

---

---

---

# November 2

In the midst of our hearts...

*My son, give attention to my words...*
*Keep them in the midst of your heart;*
*For they are life to those who find them, and health to all their flesh.*
Proverbs 4:20-22

Wow. These are some pretty hefty promises regarding God's Word to us: *life and health*. I need some of this. How about rereading the verses above again?

Yet, these are conditional promises. In the *midst of our heart* it states here. This is where God's Word is to be hidden. It doesn't say in my mind, but *in* my heart. Because, honestly, where my heart is leaning, my thoughts and actions will follow.

I write about this often, because I need the reminder so very often. It isn't rocket science. It is simply reading God's Word *from* and *for* my heart; not for head knowledge. Try it out; read and see: in the context of this passage, pour over *Proverbs 4:20-27* and experience the Holy Spirit driving His words deep. Yes. Life and health is the promise for doing so.

What Jesus is whispering to my heart today:

---

---

---

---

---

# November 3

Nope. I am not claiming to be on par with Jeremiah, the prophet...

*Thus the Lord said to me: "Go and get yourself a linen sash, and put it around your waist...arise...go to the Euphrates, and hide it there in a hole in the rock."*
Jeremiah 13:1-4

One time, about six years ago, I sensed Jesus giving me a bit-of-a-crazy thing to do. While at our family cabin, the Holy Spirit told me to go dunk myself in the lake across the road. Yep. Really. Dunk myself seven times. In sheer obedience, I did as I was told. I knew it was to break generational bondages that lingered over my family: unbelief, any addictions, rebellion, self-seeking – you name it.

Now today I remember – God's goodness and faithfulness to my family. Today my husband and oldest daughter baptized our oldest grandchild in the very same lake. One year ago yesterday, our daughter was proposed to by her Jesus-loving soon-to-be husband at the same lake. Five years ago, our only son rededicated his life to Christ in the same location.

I get that dousing yourself in a lake could be fodder for weirdness! However, when the Lord speaks to you, and what you are hearing or sensing agrees with His Written Word, be sure to follow through. Like Jeremiah, we only need to be obedient – the rest is up to Him.

What Jesus is whispering to my heart today:

_____

_____

_____

_____

_____

# November 4

Often, healing from life's hurts takes place in layers…

*I will not drive them out from before you in one year, lest the land become desolate and the beasts of the field become too numerous for you.*
Exodus 23:29

The Lord spoke these words to the nation Israel, just as they were about to conquer their enemies and enter the Promised Land. He speaks the same words to us as we seek Him to conquer our enemies of addiction, harmful behaviors, and hurts from our past. One step at a time, one layer of heartache or bondage being defeated, before the next one comes off.

Yes, Jesus can instantly deliver and heal. We all have experienced this. However, He knows, oh so wisely, that every territory of freedom we reach needs to be established by time in His felt presence and the exceeding power of His Word. As Jesus said in *Matthew 12:33-35*, if we don't fill the newly freed territories of our life with Him, the devil will likely come back seven times stronger. Hard words to hear. But true.

So don't grow discouraged in seeking your personal freedom. Partner with the Holy Spirit and firmly establish new freedoms in Him. Work with Him on your next issue that needs His deliverance and walk in the wonder of glorious liberty and life.

What Jesus is whispering to my heart today:

_____

_____

_____

_____

_____

# November 5

In my youth I really, really, *really* wanted to have straight hair...

*Not that I have already attained...but I press on, that I may lay hold of that for which Christ Jesus has also laid hold of me.*
Philippians 3:12

I grew up in the era of bell-bottoms, granny-square vests, and stick-straight hair. I am pretty sure some of you reading this don't have a clue what a granny-square vest is and would wonder who in their right mind would want to wear one. Nevertheless, having straight, long locks was the prerequisite for being considered cool.

I was far from cool. Even though I dressed the part, my hair was thick, unruly, curly, and not the most attractive shade. I straightened my hair with an iron – a clothes iron. I often had dubious scars from getting the iron too close to my forehead and armpits – don't ask. I bleached my strands into a crazy-orange tone. I duct-taped my bangs, wore curlers the size of gallon coffee-cans to bed, and endured untold teenaged angst. All for my unquenchable desire to look like Peggy Lipton from the *Mod Squad* – again, don't ask.

What is motivating our life's passion now? Really? Is it worth all that time and effort? If it isn't Jesus, it may be time to stop chasing the wind and find all that our hearts are looking for is His heart alone. We won't be disappointed. Ever.

What Jesus is whispering to my heart today:

_____

_____

_____

_____

# November 6

I want to live life in full color...

*...He who is coming after me is mightier than I...*
*He will baptize you with the Holy Spirit and fire.*
Matthew 3:11

Photography is a new hobby of mine. I use it to create Christian memes
with inspirational quotes and Bible verses. I love for the photo's colors to
be *saturated.* In other words, to be deep, rich, and full colored. I want to
live a saturated life – walking in the miraculous and glorifying Jesus.
Only the Holy Spirit can cause a meat-and-potatoes, made-of-dust life to
live this way.

The original Greek New Testament word for baptize in the verse above is
*Baptizo*: meaning to baptize, to dip, dye, immerse, plunge, submerge,
inundate, flood, swamp, soak, douse, drench, and saturate.

Ponder each one of these words in the definition. Which one pings your
heartstrings? For me now, it is *saturate.* To be so full of His Spirit I can't
absorb any more of Him until He is poured through my life to others.

Yeah. I want to live in the continual baptism of the Spirit – Book of Acts
style – in full color for Jesus.

What Jesus is whispering to my heart today:

_____
_____
_____
_____
_____

# November 7

In the midst of this week...

Should your tires be flat, your wallet is even flatter, but your tummy seems to be anything but flat, it is time to take a deep breath of the Holy Spirit, turn off all media, and run to Jesus' presence. Open His Word and drink in His life.
*Psalm 16:11*

Should your work seem daunting, your household floundering, and your peace of mind disappearing, it is time to re-surrender your life to the One and Only who can bring hope, joy, strength, and the ever-needed wisdom and calm you are lacking. He is faithful, even when you are not.
*Romans 12:1-2*

This is a week of new beginnings, hopes to be realized, and miracles to watch for. Keep your eyes open, your heart tender, and your mind from distraction. This week will be awesome in Jesus, no matter what you face, because He Who is in you is greater than anything!
*1 John 4:4*

What Jesus is whispering to my heart today:

_____

_____

_____

_____

_____

# November 8

Do you know what your soul is?

*My soul follows close behind You;*
*Your right hand upholds me.*
Psalm 63:8

I was a Christian for many years before I really knew what this major part of my being was. When my eyes were opened to what God's Word said about it in the original languages, it literally transformed my walk in Jesus.

Your soul is your mind and your heart. It is your thoughts, emotions, personality, ability to choose, and intellect. Your soul is the real you that is unseen but drives everything about your life. Yes, your thoughts and emotions go hand in hand. And the passage above is a call to follow – follow hard after, pursue, and cling to the Lord Jesus with all your heart and mind. With all of your – soul. Let that sink in.

Are your thoughts and emotions distracting you from Him? Simply set your soul completely upon Him. You will find satisfaction and healing you never thought possible before.
*Psalm 63:5, Psalm 23:3*

What Jesus is whispering to my heart today:

_____

_____

_____

_____

_____

# November 9

I love, cherish, and honor my husband, but he can be a little bit of a wild driver sometimes. And yes, this is round two of yesterday's verse...

*My soul follows close behind You;*
*Your right hand upholds me.*
Psalm 63:8

Just ask our adult kids. We are too big of a family to make it anywhere in one minivan anymore. We have to follow each other, usually Dad, to get to a desired destination. And to follow, we have to stay right on his tail, up-close and personal. When he stops, we stop. When he turns left, we turn left. Heaven forbid we lag behind, because we will surely lose sight of him.

Jesus wants us to follow Him in this manner too. Staying right on His tail. Right on His bumper. He has a wild, wonder-filled adventure for our lives that we might miss if we aren't in hot pursuit of Him. Most of us – and this was my story for too many decades – are lax about our pursuit of Him with our soul as we looked at yesterday. Then, we wonder why our lives as Christians are still so messy and powerless.

May I encourage you – and myself – to tailgate Jesus with everything we have. *John 8:12*

What Jesus is whispering to my heart today:

_____

_____

_____

_____

_____

# November 10

"I just want to know, what level of crazy are we talking about here?"

*And they went out and preached everywhere, the Lord working with them and confirming the word through the accompanying signs. Amen.*
Mark 16:20

My daughter in the faith, Jaime, and I had a good laugh today as she related a close friend's somewhat skeptical reaction to the miraculous works of Jesus that Jaime was sharing with her.

The not-quite-yet-believer queried her, *Do you believe this?* Yes, Jaime does. And yes, we laughed. Because we are just a little crazy. A little crazy about seeing the Lord transform lives, heal marriages, mend broken bodies, and set emotional captives free, just to name a few of His specialties.

So, call me crazy. But after having Stage 4 incurable cancer return for the third time three years ago, I was told I was at the end of my life. I then underwent major surgery and the cancer that had been on the PET and CScans was nowhere to be found – all because of Jesus. Well, I call that crazy-wonderful and I want to be used by Him to see more.

I love being a little bit crazy about King Jesus.

What Jesus is whispering to my heart today:

_____
_____
_____
_____
_____

# November 11

Truthfully? I am not a very good intercessor – you know, a prayer warrior...

*And he saw that there was no man, and wondered that there was no intercessor: therefore His arm brought salvation unto Him; and His righteousness, it sustained Him.*
Isaiah 59:16

The Hebrew word here for *intercessor* is **Paga**: literally, to reach for, meet up with someone, or to reach the mark of something. It all means to run after and even fall upon someone. Think tackle. A hot pursuit to grab hold of.

These terms help me. They excite me, even. Our God desires for us to ask our petitions by pursuing Him, tackling Him, and running past all boundaries into His throne room. I don't think this means intercession is hard or difficult; it is more like an invitation to join Jesus in His adventure and to blaze a path through hell for what is urgently on our hearts.

No, *intercession* for our loved ones, for circumstances, and for nations isn't difficult – it is His invitation to go deeper.

What Jesus is whispering to my heart today:

_____

_____

_____

_____

_____

# November 12

You have heard this story before: A relief agency heads into a famine-entrenched area with sacks of seed to grow life-giving crops for generations to come...

Nevertheless, the impoverished people are so starved that they tear into the bags of grain and devour them. Nothing is planted, nothing is sown, and nothing is cultivated. Life-sustaining harvests that might have fed them for years are no more.

*But he who received seed on the good ground is he who hears the word and understands it, who indeed bears fruit and produces: some a hundredfold, some sixty, some thirty.*
Matthew 13:23

This is the same for us if the only spiritual nourishment we receive is when Sunday rolls around. Our pastor's teaching from God's Word feeds us for a moment. However, because we don't sow the seed of His Word for ourselves - cultivating and nurturing it with daily attention – we are spiritually famished. We wonder why God seems far away, guidance is hard to come by, and His voice seems to be quiet.

Instead, let's stop having our only spiritual meal once a week and sow a rich harvest of His Word in our lives that will be lush and bountiful for years to come. Jesus promises: we will never be hungry.

What Jesus is whispering to my heart today:

_____

_____

_____

_____

_____

# November 13

Entertaining insecurities, sucks…

*Jesus, knowing that the Father had given all things into His hands, and that He had come from God and was going to God, rose from supper and laid aside His garments, took a towel and girded Himself.*
John 13:4

The bondage of insecurity about who we are, what we look like, or any variety of human weaknesses, can cause so much damage and loss to our lives. Honestly. Take it from one who lived most of her life ducking reality and continually living under the premise that she needed to prove her worth. A person can do stupid things when they live like I did.

Not Jesus, however. Knowing Who He was in these moments at the last supper, just before He washed the disciples' feet, gave Him the ability to be completely selfless, even to the point of the cross. He didn't hide or duck from His mission. He didn't need to prove Himself to anyone. He was absolutely secure in Who He was.

Jesus can break these dreaded strongholds and hindrances in our lives and it is time that we let Him. He can heal us and He wants to. It is time to know and live in who we really are. We are His children.

What Jesus is whispering to my heart today:

_____

_____

_____

_____

_____

# November 14

At the midst of this week...

Should *your country* seem overwhelmed, in turmoil, full of restlessness and unrest, look to the King of Kings. He is still on His throne and He is not overwhelmed, in turmoil, or unrest. In Him is no shadow of turning, and His love is unabated by world events. He knows the beginning to the end, and He is at work drawing many to Himself and giving healing and comfort to those who invite Him to come into their lives.
*James 1:17*

Should *you* be overwhelmed, in turmoil, full of restlessness and unrest, look to the Prince of Peace. If you have received Him, He is Your Rock, Your Shelter, and Your Tower of Refuge. Find genuine comfort, direction, healing, deliverance, and strength in the power of the Holy Spirit. What are you waiting for? Run to Him and don't get up until you sense His presence and receive a fresh word from His Word.
*Psalm 18:1-2*

This is a week of new beginnings, hopes to be realized, and miracles to watch for. Keep your eyes open, your heart tender, and your mind from distraction. This week will be awesome in Jesus because He Who is in you is greater than anything!
*1 John 4:4*

What Jesus is whispering to my heart today:

_____

_____

_____

_____

_____

# November 15

Reign in life. Really??

*For if by the one man's offense death reigned through the one,*
*much more those who receive abundance of grace and of the gift of*
*righteousness will reign in life through the One, Jesus Christ.*
Romans 5:17

For years I thought about:

*Getting by in life.*
*Surviving life.*
*Making it through another day in life.*

But it was never *reigning in life.*

Only Jesus. Only His abundant, powerful, lavish grace and the free gift
of His righteousness can cause a lost and weary soul to reign in life.
Even those of us who feel neither lost nor weary have to admit: life could
be better.

It can be. Invite Him in. Surrender everything to Him. Stand Back. Stand
in His grace. Let His righteousness cover you and see what He does in
and through you. You, too, can reign in life through the One and Only.

What Jesus is whispering to my heart today:

_____

_____

_____

_____

_____

# November 16

An uneven exchange…

*…He said to them, "Whoever desires to come after Me, let him deny himself, and take up his cross, and follow Me."* Mark 8:34b

We are often mistaken about what Jesus is communicating about picking up our cross. It is *not* pain, disease, suffering, torment, or loss of relationships. The cross is *not* about the hardships of living in a broken, evil, and weary world. Jesus came on a rescue mission. If we fully *trust Him* – that is the caveat here – He has made every believer more than a conqueror. His love, joy, healing, restoration, and deliverance are ours, no matter what our circumstances may be. No, the cross is explained in the verse following:

*For whoever desires to save his life will lose it, but whoever loses his life for My sake and the gospel's will save it.* Mark 8:35

*Our cross* is when we lay down our plans, dreams, and hopes – for His plans, dreams, and hopes. Our lives for His cause alone. His will be done, not ours; just as Jesus spoke to the Father as He was about to pick up His cross – *for us*.

Yet, it is an uneven exchange. Our rags for His riches. Our nothingness for His extraordinary. Our lack for His abundance. Our sin for His grace. Yes, it is an uneven exchange indeed. What are we waiting for?

What Jesus is whispering to my heart today:

_____

_____

_____

_____

# November 17

Do you ever feel less than, not enough, or lacking talent, brains, brawn, or beauty?

*...and you are complete in Him...*
Colossians 1:10a

Take a look at the definition of the original Greek New Testament word *Pleroo* used for *complete* here:

To make full, to fill up, to cram, to cause to abound, furnish, supply liberally, to fill to the top so that nothing is lacking and nothing more can be added. Full measure, to accomplish...and so much more!

Honestly. Sit in Colossians, Chapters 1-3, and have your world rocked. Genuinely ask for the Holy Spirit's revelation of what is being said here. It will take a lifetime's learning and a complete paradigm shift in our way of thinking about *everything*. Yet, it will be oh so worth it. Even at our final breath, we will only have scratched the surface of all Who Jesus is, and Who He is *in* us.

But know this truth: you are *complete* in Him! And *in Him* alone!

What Jesus is whispering to my heart today:

_____

_____

_____

_____

_____

# November 18

Other than the Lord Jesus, who are your Bible heroes or heroines?

*The Holy Spirit said to Philip, "Go over and walk along beside the carriage."* Acts 8:29 NLT

For me, in the Old Testament, I am nuts over David, Daniel, and Deborah. For the New Testament, I am crazy about Peter, John, Anna, and Philip. Yes, these are my go-to peeps.

Let's take Philip. Read the major account of his life found in Acts 8. Honestly. He was just a regular, meat-and-potatoes kind of guy. He was one of Jesus' disciples, but not in the inner circle. I kind of think he had a laid-back, sunbaked, surfer mentality. Someone I can relate to.

Yet here he is in the Scriptures, hearing the Holy Spirit speak direction, acting upon it, by leading a high official to Jesus, baptizing the guy, then having a Holy Spirit supernatural transport take place! I want to be a Philip. I want to continually aspire to hear the Spirit and obey. I want to see my life be used to bring others to Christ. And, I want to continually walk in the miraculous. You too?

Let's *do* this. Jesus is waiting and a weary world needs to meet Him through Philips, like you and me.

What Jesus is whispering to my heart today:

_____

_____

_____

_____

_____

# November 19

This verse from the Amplified Bible Version did something for my soul recently...

*The Lord God is my Strength, my personal bravery, and my invincible army; He makes my feet like hinds' feet and will make me to walk – not to stand still in terror, but to walk – and make spiritual progress upon my high places of trouble, suffering, or responsibility!*
Habakkuk 3:19 AMPC

This verse from the minor prophet – whose name no one seems to know how to pronounce – hits the nail on the head. The phrases that spoke to me personally were: *He is my personal bravery* and *spiritual progress...upon my responsibility*. The day I read this I was feeling the heat of personal challenge and overwhelming responsibility about two matters in my life. However, God's Word annihilated that daunting feeling I was about to come under. And, Jesus did come through for me – in both areas I was facing.

So how about you? What is the Holy Spirit whispering to your heart from His Word? Receive what He is saying, make it your own, believe it with all of your heart, and *trust, trust, trust* His promises to you.

What Jesus is whispering to my heart today:

_____

_____

_____

_____

_____

# November 20

I have so much to be thankful for...

*Let everything that has breath praise the LORD. Praise the LORD!*
Psalm 150:6

This week of Thanksgiving, let's praise Him *'til the cows come home.* Let's wake up thankful. Let's go through the day blessing Jesus with our love and gratitude. Let's get on our knees before bed tonight and have a praise fest.

I had a trying day. You too? Not horrible, just stuff. But you know what? God is worthy to be praised. And when I get my thankfulness on...the doors of heaven open wide and the Holy Spirit causes me to soar.

The enemy loves nothing more than for us to get our eyes on ourselves and our circumstances, and off the One and Only. So join me these next few days, months, and years. Let's look up and lift up our hands because there is overflowing joy and power in an *actively grateful* heart.

What Jesus is whispering to my heart today:

_____
_____
_____
_____
_____

# November 21

In the midst of this week...

Should your dog eat your slippers, your favorite team bite the dust, or you just plain feel like the stuff of your life is insurmountable, look to the One who holds all the answers. He never promised life would be easy in this broken, evil world, but He did promise that you are more than a conqueror when you abide in Him. He delivers on His promises.
*Romans 8:37*

Should your relationships be frayed and worn, and impatience and frustration are tempting you, look at yourself first. Don't place blame. It takes two-to-tango, as the saying goes. Jesus always tells us to take the splinter out of our own eye first before even attempting to point out the log in another's eye. Let Jesus deal with your issues. That's what He is asking of you in this moment.
*Matthew 7:3*

This is a week of new beginnings, hopes to be realized, and miracles to watch for. Keep your eyes open, your heart tender, and your mind from distraction. This week will be awesome in Jesus because He Who is in you is greater than anything!
*1 John 4:4*

What Jesus is whispering to my heart today:

_____

_____

_____

_____

_____

# November 22

Sometimes family holidays aren't that much fun…

*God sets the solitary in families;*
*He brings out those who are bound into prosperity;*
*But the rebellious dwell in a dry land.*
Psalm 68:6

Some of us are recently – or not so recently-divorced.
Some of us have lost someone dear.
Some of us have, well, whacked-out families.

I mean really. Sometimes holidays are difficult at best. However, God sees. He knows and He is always on the side of the lonely. He knows you can be in a crowd and still be alone.

Wherever the coming holidays find you, or for the next big event that appears on your calendar, look up to your Heavenly Father. Feel the embrace of the Son and the Comfort of the Holy Spirit. He is real, His presence tangible, and His love is more than enough.

What Jesus is whispering to my heart today:

_____

_____

_____

_____

_____

# November 23

Oh, give thanks to the Lord!

*Your love, LORD, reaches to the heavens,*
*your faithfulness to the skies.*
Psalm 36:5

At work yesterday, we last stragglers who didn't take the day off, asked each other how we were spending the holiday. You know – who is cooking, what is being cooked, and how many will be feasting. Of course, everyone groaned when I shared that Randy and I would be driving 400 miles to Los Angeles right after work. Traffic, traffic, traffic!

Nevertheless, the bottom line for me is: I am so thankful for *everything* in my life. I told Randy the other night after receiving another clear CTscan report – I don't ever want to be like the nine healed lepers who didn't come back to Jesus and worship. I resolve to be more grateful every single day I draw breath. Really.

It is the only way to live, even when stuff isn't yet resolved. He has never failed me yet and His love and faithfulness are without end. I can trust Jesus with everything. I choose to do so with praise on my lips and my hands upraised. Will you join me?

What Jesus is whispering to my heart today:

_____

_____

_____

_____

_____

# November 28

In the midst of this week…

If your kids are whining, your workmates are irritating, and the neighbors won't mow their lawn, it is probably a sign your soul is running on empty! It is time to get filled up, saturated, and doused in the Holy Spirit. Get alone with the Lord and His Word, rest in His presence, and get fueled up to greet the week ahead.
*Psalm 63:1-2*

If you feel burnt out, stressed out, or wiped out – again, it is time to return to the living waters of the Holy Spirit. Are you unsure about His work in you? It is time to spend some time getting to know Who He is. Take a look at the Gospel of *John, Chapters 14, 15,* and *16*. Don't remain a desert when you can become an oasis.

This is a week of new beginnings, hopes to be realized, and miracles to watch for. Keep your eyes open, your heart tender, and your mind from distraction. This week will be awesome in Jesus because He Who is in you is greater than anything!
1 John 4:4

What Jesus is whispering to my heart today:

_____
_____
_____
_____
_____

# November 29

I grew up not far from the theme park affectionately called *The Happiest Place on Earth...*

*These things I have spoken to you, that My joy may remain in you, and that your joy may be full.*
John 15:11

Truly, it *is* a very happy and wonder-filled destination. However, the problem lies when I exit this theme park's gates and wave goodbye to Mickey. I cannot take the park home with me. This *Happy Place* is not there for me when tragedy strikes, calamity calls, and confusion reigns.

Jesus is *always* there for me. His promised joy is *always* my portion. Yet why did I used to spend so much time feeling unsatisfied – that life was mundane, and my heart feeling flat – even in the best of circumstances? The reason lies in the verses beforehand in *John 15*: *Abiding, remaining, dwelling, and feasting in the Vine.*

Dwelling in Jesus' presence is my life anthem. Honestly, you can read it in everything I write. Time alone with Him, drinking in His presence, saturating in His Word, and experiencing the power of the Holy Spirit, is cause for joy that carries one through life's most trying storms. I am selfish enough that I don't ever want to lose or forfeit His joy – I lived too long the other way, and I won't ever go back.

What Jesus is whispering to my heart today:

_____

_____

_____

_____

_____

# November 30

Peter's words give us the recipe for Spirit-filled, extraordinary, and effervescent living. And, first on the list is *repentance...*

*Repent therefore and be converted, that your sins may be blotted out, so that times of refreshing may come from the presence of the Lord.*
Acts 3:19

I was truly amazed a few years ago when I studied this word, *repentance:*

*Metanoeo* Greek, meaning: From *Meta* a change of place or condition; and *Noeo* to exercise the mind, think, comprehend. To think differently. To undergo a moral change of direction.

Repentance is a paradigm shift in the way *I think* and not so much about what *I do*. Trying to break my own sin-bondages – the stuff that messes me up – by trying to change my actions, is pointless. Has it ever worked for you? When my mind is transformed – seeking God's viewpoint first, not the world's way or my own skewed thinking – then and only then, am I transformed. Hmm...didn't Paul say this in *Romans 12:1-2?*

To know His thoughts, I need to know His Word and His vocabulary: love, mercy, grace, freedom, abundance, goodness, truth, life – the list goes on and on. When I let the Spirit do a total thought over-haul in me, then the rivers of living water from God's presence flood in; refreshing, restoring, rejuvenating, and revealing His life in me. Ahhh, yes!

What Jesus is whispering to my heart today:

_____

_____

_____

_____

# December 1

Silent Night. Holy Night...

When our Savior entered the world as a wee babe – fully God and fully man – He was entering enemy territory.

*For we do not wrestle against flesh and blood, but against principalities, against powers, against the rulers of the darkness of this age, against spiritual hosts of wickedness in the heavenly places.*
Ephesians 6:12

Jesus' walk upon earth was a rescue mission and things haven't changed since He first came. In this passage, we hear the urgency in the Apostle Paul's voice for the church to wake up. To put on the armor of God and do battle against the enemy. *Not* against people.

How quickly I get my eyes on stuff, situations, and yes, others, when the real conflict is against demon hordes and the enemy himself? Yet, Jesus has called us to be an army that battles – *on our knees.*

What are you facing? Who are you directing your anger, anguish, or irritation towards? It might be time to let the Holy Spirit reveal what is really going on and who the real culprit is. Then and only then, real victory can be secured in Jesus' Name.

What Jesus is whispering to my heart today:

_____

_____

_____

_____

_____

# December 2

Small. Small things. Small packages...

*A little one shall become a thousand, And a small one a strong nation.*
*I, the Lord, will hasten it in its time.*
Isaiah 60:22

For years, I despaired that what I had to offer the Lord was too small. For years I despaired that I was too small. Yes, I despaired, compared, and felt defeated. Yet, our Heavenly Father apparently delights in tiny, little, and small things.

So, if this season finds you fretting about the size of your abilities, your home, your income, your ministry, your influence, or yourself, remember…

To God, profoundly significant things come in small packages. We need only look at the baby in the manger to see the size of His heart and what He can do with the small things we surrender to Him.

What Jesus is whispering to my heart today:

_____

_____

_____

_____

_____

# December 3

A verse found in the Christmas story has been a key of wonder for me…

*Blessed is she who believed, for there will be a fulfillment of those things which were told her from the Lord.*
Luke 1:45

Not that I have lived up to these words. Nevertheless, they embody the great truth that *faith* is ever so important to the Lord Jesus.

We can sing His praise, we can dance in worship, and we can shout in jubilation in His presence. We can go to church every Sunday, read our Bibles daily, and share the gospel, but – oh my – without *faith* it is impossible to please Him *Hebrews 11:6*.

I know, we walk timidly around this subject not wanting to offend or hurt anyone, so I am not looking at others as I write. I am talking to myself and remembering the power of the angel's words to Mary.

Whatever our place of current struggle, let's choose to believe His Word despite what we are feeling. Emotions *will follow* our choice. Let's ask for His help with our unbelief, because the fulfilment of much of what He wants to give, do, and have take place in our lives hinges upon what we believe. No, this not a type of *works* to earn merit, but the Lord loves it when we *trust* Him.

What Jesus is whispering to my heart today:

_____

_____

_____

_____

_____

# December 4

I love Christmas trees. My husband and I purchased two trees yesterday, and yes, they are beautiful and gorgeous. One is located in the room where I meet with the Lord every morning…

*…for the Lord does not see as man sees; for man looks at the outward appearance, but the Lord looks at the heart."*
1 Samuel 16:7b

In the candlelight – for the trees are yet unadorned – I could see that someone had come along and snipped several branches just so the tree would have a perfect shape. Hmmm. I'll bet the tree was even more beautiful in its original, natural wildness. Why does man – namely me – put such emphasis on appearance? On tidying everything up? Making it *perfect?*

All this to say – Jesus was born in a cattle stall. A pretty wild birthing room if there ever was one. So, He probably isn't as interested in my face being on the pages of *Vogue* or my home being photographed in *Architectural Digest*. He is more interested in the direction of my *heart.*

I want to be wild for Jesus. I want to be all that *He* has designed for me rather than my being so concerned about the *outside*. Instead, I want to Him to heal me on the inside, so that I am free to serve and love Him with abandon and without the fear of appearance.

What Jesus is whispering to my heart today:

_____

_____

_____

_____

_____

# December 5

In the midst of this busy, crazy, wonder-filled Christmas-time week...

Should you grow weary, tired, impatient, or just plain *done* – remember
Mary. She was having a rough go about this time too. Nevertheless, her
trust was in the One who loved her beyond reason.
*Luke 2:5*

Should you feel like you aren't enough, have enough, or do enough –
consider the shepherds. Their job was pretty much out-of-site, out-of-the-
limelight, and out-of-reach from the nearest paparazzi. Yet, God *chose*
them to be the bearers and witnesses of the Savior's birth. He sees you,
too!
*Luke 2:8-15*

This is a week of new beginnings, hopes to be realized, and miracles to
watch for. Keep your eyes open, your heart tender, and your mind from
distraction. This week will be awesome in Jesus because He Who is in
you is greater than anything!
*1 John 4:4*

What Jesus is whispering to my heart today:

_____

_____

_____

_____

_____

# December 10

Do you ever feel like a broken, crumbly gingerbread-man cookie?

*Be anxious for nothing, but in everything by prayer and supplication, with thanksgiving, let your requests be made known to God*
Philippians 4:6

I mean really. The Christmas season can be the most stressful, anxious, lonely, aggravating, or depressing time of the year. Do you fall into any of these categories today? Do you think this is His plan for you?

No, of course not. And for me as well. Time to calm down. Time to take a deep breath of the Holy Spirit and drink in His presence with some quiet. Even when the to-do list is yelling my name from the kitchen counter. I don't want live a broken-cookie-style life – feeling like my head has fallen off somewhere or my arm needs to be pasted back on with icing. I choose to live in the promise of the next verse:

*...and the peace of God, which surpasses all understanding, will guard your hearts and minds through Christ Jesus.* Philippians 4:7

To receive this gift of peace, I have to let anxiety go, pray about everything, and praise Him in the midst of the craziness. If I do, you know what? This will be the best Christmas – *ever.*

What Jesus is whispering to my heart today:

_____

_____

_____

_____

_____

# December 11

I realize that a devotional blog doesn't usually talk about Macy's, however...

The store was packed. The store was beautiful. And there were wall-to-wall people. I was meeting my husband at a designated time in a designated place.

By some minor miracle, I arrived first. There were tons of shoppers hustling and bustling behind me as I stopped to look at something. Then I heard someone clearing their throat. I distinguished this small sound amid the overhead music, the customers around me, and the employees talking. I knew it was Randy. He was about twenty feet behind me. In all that din of chatter, I heard him.

*But He who enters by the door is the shepherd of the sheep. To him the doorkeeper opens, and the sheep hear His voice; and He calls His own sheep by name and leads them out.*
 John 10:2-3

I want to hear the Lord's voice that way too. I want to know Him so intimately that all He needs to do is clear His throat in the midst of the noise of life. And I answer His call.

What Jesus is whispering to my heart today:

_____

_____

_____

_____

_____

# December 16

I *love* Christmas time...

*For you know the grace of our Lord Jesus Christ, that though He was*
*rich, yet for your sakes He became poor, that you through His poverty*
*might become rich.*
2 Corinthians 8:9

I love the trees. I love the lights. I love the sparkle. I love the music. I
love the fragrance of pine. I love the sweet delight of a crazy house full
of family. Most of all, I *love* the wonder.

The verse above is unfathomable. Though He was rich, He became poor.
The God of the Universe became man to rescue me. And you. This is the
story of Christmas. So, in all the festivities, someone you know might
need to be rescued, too. Be sensitive to those around you and the Holy
Spirit calling to their hearts. And while you are at it, be sensitive to His
calling to *you* as He continues the riches of His rescue in your life as
well. I will do the same.

What wonder.

What Jesus is whispering to my heart today:

_____

_____

_____

_____

_____

# December 17

No joke. I am 99.9% sure I encountered a real angel last year at Christmas at my workplace...

*Do not forget to entertain strangers, for by so doing some have unwittingly entertained angels.*
Hebrews 13:2

Last Christmas Eve, I was alone in the office when a scraggly man appeared at my door. Oh my, now what? This older, rag-tag man with the most piercing blue eyes told me how he was caring for his elderly mom and needed my help *THAT DAY*. The verse above immediately came to my mind. I knew the Holy Spirit was speaking to me to shape up because someone special was in front of me. Yes, really.

I was cranky. Yet, I tried to help him. The situation kept getting worse with more hoops for me to jump through to get him the aid he was requiring. Then, it became laughable. I just knew this was the *real deal*. The Lord has a sense of humor – *for sure*. When everything finally came to a close, the man took my hand, looked me straight in the eye, and said to me – *You are a real angel*.

So this Christmas, and every other day of the year, slow down and take notice. You never know. You may be entertaining an angel sent from heaven, or you may be their *God-sent angel*.

What Jesus is whispering to my heart today:

_____

_____

_____

_____

_____

# December 18

Christmas is in full swing and my to-do list is still a mile long...

*You have endowed him with eternal blessings*
*and given him the joy of Your presence.*
Psalm 21:6 NLT

I had sweet quiet time with the Lord before work this morning. While still there in that peaceful place, I started my list of stuff to do. It went on and on and on. Do you know what I mean?

I heard the whisper of the Holy Spirit: *Let Me orchestrate this Christmas season.* For once, I didn't question. Yep, I want to really enjoy this oh so short season in His presence. The desire for the *eternal* to trump my *to-dos.* Yes, I need to go to work, get lights on the trees, and buy presents. However, I am going to let Him call the plays. Want to join me in trusting Him for this season?

You know what? I forgot my list when I walked out the door.

Honestly. I feel great *relief.*

What Jesus is whispering to my heart today:

_____

_____

_____

_____

_____

# December 19

In the midst of this Christmas week…

If you have become over-scheduled, overwhelmed, or over-the-top nuts with stuff to do and no time to do it – take a breath, breathe a prayer, and stop. Be grateful for the One who came as a little babe to give His all that we might live. For He alone is worthy…
*John 3:16*

Should you have anxious thoughts, remember Joseph from the Christmas story. God told him exactly what to do and gave him the grace to do it. So, rehearse in your thoughts and prayers – *GOD knows what is best, perfect, and extraordinary for my life!*
*Ephesians 3:20*

This is the Eve of new beginnings, hopes to be realized, and miracles to watch for. Keep your eyes open, your heart tender, and your mind from distraction. This Christmas will be awesome in Jesus because He Who is in you is greater than anything!
*1 John 4:4*

What Jesus is whispering to my heart today:

_____

_____

_____

_____

_____

# December 20

Today I was thinking about *snow.*

*"Come now, and let us reason together," Says the LORD,*
*"Though your sins are like scarlet, They shall be as white as snow;*
*Though they are red like crimson, They shall be as wool."*
Isaiah 1:18

Take it from one who was so caught up in strongholds of guilt, and shame for most of her adult life. Knowing that He saw me *white as snow* was a game changer.

Truly believing, even if it is by baby steps, that we are completely forgiven is our foundation for moving forward in Jesus. The "No Longer Guilty" banner over our lives is the launching pad to greater freedom, knowing His will, seeing the enemy defeated, and best of all, sweeter intimacy with the Lord.

Guilt is from the pit. If you have received Jesus as your Lord and Savior, you too are white as snow and clothed in His righteousness. It is time to speak God's Word over your life and not trust your feelings. What a Christmas gift!

What Jesus is whispering to my heart today:

_____

_____

_____

_____

_____

# December 21

I received an early Christmas present about two months ago...

*He also brought me out into a broad place;*
*He delivered me because He delighted in me.*
Psalm 18:19

Jesus delivered me from a lifetime bondage...

I can't take the time to share how He accomplished this or how I was set free in layers, nevertheless. I now know that I am completely free to be seen *only by Him*.

I think a lot of us need this gift. We need not only to know we are seen by Him, but to know in the depths of our being that He is *the only One* who needs to see us. He is more than enough. I am wondering if this struggle to be known and seen is a part of the *selfie* craze.

Anyway, please pray about this. Let Jesus give you an extraordinary Christmas gift as well.

What Jesus is whispering to my heart today:

_____

_____

_____

_____

_____

# December 22

There is a line from a Christmas carol that *wrecks* me every time...

*Til He appeared...and the soul felt its worth.*

I, for one, spent many years feeling worthless. Never mind my adoring parents and joyful childhood. My self-loathing was a product of simply being born into a broken, fallen world which the enemy of my soul rules. I masked this self-loathing in a cloak of pride, but that is another story. The wonder of it is – Jesus set me free from the tyranny of this lie regarding my worth and continues to release me from its grip.

*Jesus came for the sick...the sick at heart.*
Mark 2:17

I have met people – many people – who think their self-sufficiency is all they need. They really do seem to have it altogether. I am afraid for these people. I am afraid they will miss what He has for them. I am afraid they will never learn that He can carry the load and they don't have to prove anything anymore. Is this you?

What a relief to know He is everything. And what joy it is for me to know: this messed up girl is now the most valuable thing in His heart. And, you are too.

What Jesus is whispering to my heart today:

_____

_____

_____

_____

_____

# December 23

I should have been a shepherd...

*Now there were in the same country shepherds living out in the fields, keeping watch over their flock by night.*
Luke 2:8

I am told that the shepherd jobs went to the very young or the very old. Maybe those with not too much smarts, or those who preferred lambs to being with people. I would have been perfect for the job.

I would love to have been with the crew out in the fields surrounding Bethlehem that cold, dark night. The good news of Jesus was first preached to these not-so-esteemed ones. This gives me hope. It also knocks *pride* out of me. Jesus works when *I know* I have nothing to offer anyone without His touch. This is what I learn from these humble-position folks.

Ironically, Jesus *has* caused me to be a shepherd – a shepherd of people. I receive this calling with great joy. It has been an honor to preach the gospel, God's Word, and the power of the Holy Spirit to His lambs.

So what has He called you to do? Whatever it is, you and I together need to remember the shepherds in the field. We will always serve Jesus best when we realize that we are nothing without Him.

What Jesus is whispering to my heart today:

_____

_____

_____

_____

_____

# December 28

This last week of the year is a good time to reflect upon our lives...

*But we all, with unveiled face,*
*beholding as in a mirror the glory of the Lord, are being transformed*
*into the same image from glory to glory,*
*just as by the Spirit of the Lord.*
2 Corinthians 3:18

Really. Especially as a Jesus Follower, I have to ask myself: Did I allow Him to do His healing work in my heart, mind, and body this past year? Have I journeyed a bit further down the road of faith by knowing Him more intimately? Do I look a little bit more like Him? Did I leave eternal footprints this past year? You know, were the people around me impacted by the Holy Spirit because I was in their midst?

This isn't guilt and condemnation time. When has that ever worked? It is more like, I-don't-want-to-waste-another-minute-time. Take it from someone who wasted a *lot* of minutes and years, but hit the reset button with Jesus some time ago and has been enjoying the thrill-ride with Him ever since.

Let's take a moment and look Jesus fully in the face and let the Spirit's transformation of our lives continue full-steam-ahead.

What Jesus is whispering to my heart today:

_____

_____

_____

_____

_____

# December 29

As we prepare for the New Year – let's listen for the Lord to possibly awaken something creative in each of us

*In the beginning God created the heavens and the earth.*
Genesis 1:1

Every one of us have a creative bent. You know, something we like to do, something we make, or something we form. Maybe we are secretly passionate about building, writing, cooking, dancing, any type of media or art. Something that would bring us great pleasure, but we are afraid to try because we might come up short. Or worse yet, we are hesitant or held back due to the fear we might fail.

We think: Why bother? Who will see? Who will care?

He does.

What have you given up on or never tried because you thought the *why* questions? I think our creative God created us in His image for His pleasure and ours. Let His gifts be revived in you again this coming year. These desires to create are His Christmas gift to you...

What Jesus is whispering to my heart today:

_____

_____

_____

_____

_____